GOOD NEWS STUDIES

Consulting Editor: Robert J. Karris, O.F.M.

Volume 7

A New Look
at
Preaching

Editor

John Burke, O.P.

Michael Glazier, Inc.
Wilmington, Delaware

First published in 1983 by Michael Glazier, Inc.
1723 Delaware Avenue, Wilmington, Delaware 19806
and Veritas Publications, 7-8 Lower Abbey Street, Dublin, Ireland

Library of Congress Catalog Card Number: 83-81379
International Standard Book Number:
  Good News Studies: 0-89453-290-1
  A NEW LOOK AT PREACHING
    0-89453-336-3 (Michael Glazier, Inc.)
    0-86217-074-5 (Veritas Publications)

Typography by Richard Rein Smith

Printed in the United States of America

Contents

The Contributors

Edward K. Braxton did his graduate studies at the Catholic University of Louvain. As a priest in the Archdiocese of Chicago, he has devoted much time to the renewal of theology on a pastoral level. He has contributed to leading scholarly journals such as *Harvard Theological Review* and *Theological Studies* and is an expert on the theology of Bernard Lonergan.

Raymond E. Brown, S.S., is Auburn Professor of Biblical Studies at Union Theological Seminary in New York City. Internationally renowned and respected as a biblical scholar, Father Brown's published works have had a pioneering and salutary influence on scriptural studies on the academic, ecumenical and pastoral levels. His many books reflect his abiding love and profound respect for the Scriptures, the Church, and the Christian people. Among his many published works are *The Gospel According to John* (in the *Anchor Bible*); *Crises Facing the Church;* and *The Birth of the Messiah.*

Walter J. Burghardt, S.J., is Theologian in Residence at Georgetown University and Editor in Chief of *Theological Studies*. A noted patristic scholar, he is General Editor of *Ancient Christian Writers* series. Known as the preacher's preacher, his published homilies *Tell the Next Generation* and *Sir, We Would Like to See Jesus* are models of pertinent pastoral erudition and literary finesse. His latest work is *Seasons That Laugh or Weep.*

John Burke, O.P., the editor of this book, is Executive Director of the Word of God Institute. Prior to joining the Dominican Order, he was associate director in network television with the National Broadcasting Company. He received his doctorate in theology from Catholic University. Apart from his theological work, he is well known as a preacher and as a teacher of homiletics. Among his many publications are *Gospel Power: Toward the Revitalization of Preaching* and *The Sunday Homily*.

Fred B. Craddock is Professor of Preaching and New Testament in the Candler School of Theology at Emory University. Distinguished as a scholar and as a preacher, Dr. Craddock has lectured widely and is very active in the affairs of the Christian Church (Disciples of Christ) in which he is an ordained minister. Among his publications are *Overhearing the Gospels* and *John*.

Elisabeth Schüssler Fiorenza is Professor of New Testament Studies and Theology at the University of Notre Dame. Her wide scholarship is reflected in the scope of her exegetical writings. She is well known for her scriptural and theological studies on the role of women in the church. Among her publications are *In Memory of Her: A Feminist Theological Reconstruction of Christian Origins* and *Proclamation Commentary: Series B Lent*.

James A. Forbes, Jr., Brown and Sockman Associate Professor of Preaching at Union Theological Seminary in New York, has previously taught at Union Theological Seminary in Richmond, Virginia and at Virginia Union University School of Theology. His writings and lectures are marked by a dedicated concern for a quality and relevance in the preached word to meet needs of the urban Christian today.

William J. Hill, O.P., holds his doctorate in theology from the University of St. Thomas in Rome. He is Professor of Systematic Theology at Catholic University in Washington; and is also Editor in Chief of *The Thomist*. Among his publications are *Knowing the Unknown God* and *The Three-Personed God*.

Leander E. Keck is Winkley Professor of Biblical Theology at Yale University and Dean of Yale Divinity School. He has also taught at Wellesley College, Vanderbilt Divinity School and Emory University. Dean Keck is much appreciated as a lecturer in this country and abroad. His concern for biblical preaching is manifest in his books, which include *The Bible in the Pulpit* and *Paul and His Letters.*

James M. Reese, O.S.F.S., is an Associate Professor of Theology at St. John's University in New York City. He is a member of the editorial staff of *The Bible Today* and *Biblical Theology Bulletin,* and has worked with continuing education programs for clergy and religious. Among his recent publications are *1 & 2 Thessalonians* in the *New Testament Message* series and *The Book of Wisdom, Song of Songs* in the *Old Testament Message* series.

Gerard S. Sloyan is Professor of Religion (New Testament Thought) at Temple University in Philadelphia. Ordained as a priest of the Diocese of Trenton in 1944, he has been a constructive contributor in liturgical, biblical and theological studies over the years. His interest in preaching is reflected in his many published works, among which is *A Commentary on the New Lectionary.* His latest book, *Preaching the Lectionary Readings,* will be published by Fortress Books.

Introduction

John Burke, O.P.

The chapters in this volume are the addresses and responses delivered at the First National Ecumenical Scriptural-Theological Symposium on Preaching, convened at Emory University by the Word of God Institute in celebration of its tenth anniversary of apostolic service in the renewal of preaching. Church leaders from a number of Christian denominations gathered at Emory University's Cannon Chapel to share the insights and experiences flowing from their diverse ecclesial traditions regarding the contemporary ministry of preaching in America.

Each participant had been personally invited to the Symposium. Each had contributed in some way to the formation of others in the Christian faith; they were preachers, scholars, authors, theologians, educators, ministers of the Gospel. They assembled to listen to outstanding presenters and their respondents; afterwards, each participant had the opportunity to dialogue with the speakers so that the Symposium as a whole could arrive at new insights concerning the ministry of preaching in the twentieth century.

The purpose of the Symposium, as originally conceived by the Word of God Institute, was to provide an opportunity for Church leaders to explore in some depth the dimensions of the preaching ministry, which is often thought of only in terms of Sunday preaching.

11

The Symposium concluded with an Implementation Session; its purpose was to discuss ways of communicating the insights generated by the Symposium to the respective Churches. The dynamics of this Session were unexpected but significant.

The Implementation Session was marked by theological diversity, personal anguish, pastoral frustration and ecclesial disaffection. Some of the interventions were actively hostile, revealing extreme dissatisfaction with the present situation in preaching. There was particular resentment voiced against the exclusion of women and lay persons from the effective preaching ministry. The focus of attention shifted dramatically from concern with the content of preaching to advocacies concerning who should preach and how. Indeed, one participant accused the Symposium of trying to patch up an out-moded form of Gospel communication — preaching — instead of encouraging the development of new and effective forms. Another called for the abandonment of static proclamation for a dynamic dialogic process of communication.

The disaffection that marked this final Session revealed poignantly the extent of the problem facing the contemporary Church in its efforts to spread the Gospel. The participants were devoted Christians, dedicated above the average to service, eager to proclaim and fervent in their faith in Jesus Christ. They were not alienated from either the Church or religion; they were not hostile to God nor ignorant of religious traditions, thought and language. On the contrary, they had gathered at great personal expense in terms of both time and money to share faith, grow in their undestanding of the Gospel and the nature of the preaching ministry. They were willing to sit at the feet of others in order to receive from acknowledged teachers the fruits of their scholarship.

Furthermore, they had been stimulated, refreshed, renewed and enthused; yet, at the end, many were frustrated and discouraged about the possibilities for revitalizing the Church's ministry of preaching.

What happened in the Implementation Session forces us

to ask: How do we carry on the preaching ministry in a Church in rapid, even violent, transition? How do we make the Gospel relevant to a modern world which has undergone more change in a brief thirty years than the whole human race has experienced in all its history? The rise and fall of civilizations over the centuries cannot compare with the impact on human life of the atomic age and the recent advances in science and technology.

The Gospel we proclaim is couched in the time-conditioned, culturally limited language of middle-east people; it has been modified by centuries of European thought, reflective of the comings and goings of civilizations and their struggles for survival. The problem of communicating the perennial message of the Gospel in the context of changing societies has had to have been addressed by each generation. Now it is our turn.

The need for a renewal in the communication of the Gospel was made vividly clear when the Catholic Church, in spite of all its centuries of formative influence in Christian Europe, was powerless to prevent the horror and devastation of the Second World War. That war saw destruction of lives and property unparalleled in the entire history of the world. Yet, for all its good intentions, the Church was ineffective, and its voice was so weak it was neither heard nor heeded.

Pope John XXIII, in his Opening Message to the Second Vatican Council, put into stark relief the necessity of the Church to speak in a language which would have an impact on the lives of men and women living today in a complex and, in many ways, frightening world. He said:

> The greatest concern of the Ecumenical Council is this: that the sacred deposit of Christian doctrine should be guarded and taught more efficaciously... The Church should never depart from the sacred patrimony of truth received from the Fathers; but, at the same time, she must ever look to the present, to new conditions and new forms of life introduced into the modern world, which have opened new avenues to the Catholic Apostolate.

The council Fathers themselves took up the urgency of the Pope's Message and summed up the purpose of the Council in these memorable words of their own Opening Message:

> We wish to inquire how we ought to renew ourselves, so that we may be found increasingly faithful to the Gospel of Jesus Christ. We shall take pains so to present to the men (and women) of this age God's truth in its integrity and purity that they may understand it and gladly assent to it.

The importance of relating the Gospel to contemporary society is further developed in the various decrees of the Council itself. For example, the Decree on the Bishops' Pastoral Office in the Church (*Christus Dominus*), Number 13, says:

> The bishops should present Christian doctrine in a manner adapted to the needs of the times, that is to say, in a manner corresponding to the difficulties and problems by which people are most vexatiously burdened and troubled.

At the time of the Council, theologians were arriving at new understandings of the meaning of relevancy. It was no longer enough to find words that enable the Gospel to be intellectually grasped by contemporary listeners. The Church was becoming increasingly sensitive to the need to go beyond the dissemination of information to establish bonds of friendship and solidarity with those to whom the Gospel was being addressed.

Between 1964 and 1975 Pope Paul VI issued two documents which gave eloquent voice to his own persona sensitivity to this issue. His first encyclical, *Ecclesiam Suam*, contained these words:

> Before speaking it is necessary to listen — not only to a man's voice, but to his heart... In the very act of trying to make ourselves pastors, fathers and teachers of men, we must make ourselves their brothers. The spirit of dialogue is friendship; even more, it is service. (No. 90)

His Apostolic Exhortation on Evangelization in the Modern World (*Evangelii Nuntiandi*) expands his understanding of this teaching and its importance. He writes:

> Modern man listens more willingly to witnesses than to teachers, and if he does listen to teachers, it is because they are witnesses. (No. 41)

However important dogmatic formulations may be for preserving the integrity of Christian doctrine, Paul VI insists that the effective communication of the Gospel demands a personal investment in both the experience of revelation and the lives of the listeners. Mere knowledge is not adequate to the task. He says: "In the long run, is there any other way of handing on the Gospel than by transmitting to another person one's personal experience of faith?" (No. 46)

This renewed, sensitive and adapted communication of the Gospel is not on the periphery of the Church's life; it constitutes the Church's very reason for existence. Therefore, the current teaching of the Church places communication as the primary work of the Church. The first two documents promulgated by the Second Vatican Council reflect this primacy of communication, for they are the Decree on the Instruments of Social Communication and the Constitution on the Sacred Liturgy.

The latter document is the end result of a period of intense growth in the appreciation of the centrality of the word of God in the life of the Church during the sixteen years between the issuance of *Mediator Dei* in 1947 by Pope Pius XII and the promulgation of the Constitution on the Sacred Liturgy in 1963 by the Second Vatican Council.

In *Mediator Dei*, the last important document of liturgical reform before the Second Vatican Council, the sermon was not even an integral part of the Mass. It was only an ornament or decoration "enhancing the majesty of the Great Sacrifice" like vestments and sacred rites (Article 101). It could be omitted rather easily and frequently was. In fact, it was easier to dispense with the sermon than with the candles at Eucharistic celebrations.

For the Constitution on the Sacred Liturgy, on the other hand, not only is the sermon an integral part of all liturgical celebrations, but preaching of the Gospel necessarily precedes and makes possible the celebration of all liturgy. Article 9 of the Constitution says:

> Before men can come to the liturgy, they must be called to faith and to conversion.....Therefore, the Church announces the good tidings of salvation to those who do not believe, so that all men may know the true God and Jesus Christ whom he has sent. To believers also the Church must ever preach ... to prepare them for the sacraments and all the works of charity, piety and the apostolate.

Hence, today the Church affirms that preaching is the primary ministry of its ministers and its people. Decree after decree from the Second Vatican Council stresses this fact. For bishops, Article 12 of the Decree on the Bishops' Pastoral Office in the Church (*Christus Dominus*) states that preaching is eminent among their chief duties. The Decree on the Ministry and Life of Priests (*Presbyterorum Ordinis*), Article 4, acknowledges that the proclamation of the Gospel of God to all is the primary duty of priests. Furthermore, the Decree on the Apostolate of the Laity (*Apostolicam Actuositatem*), Article 16, declares:

> Lay people too have an apostolate of the word when they announce Christ, explain and spread his teaching according to their situation and ability and faithfully profess it.

The need for the explicit articulation of the Gospel message by the laity in words as well as by example is stressed in the Decree on the Missionary Activity of the Church (*Ad Gentes*), Article 11. It asserts:

> All Christians are bound to show forth by the example of their lives and by the witness of their speech that new man which they put on at baptism and that power of the Holy Spirit by whom they were strengthened at confirmation.

As a result of the Second Vatican Council, the Roman Catholic Church has been directing its attention more emphatically to the central role preaching plays in the life of both individual Christians and the Church as a whole. Yet, the Church has still to experience the revitalization of preaching and communication that the Council envisioned and mandated. Some recent research indicates, in the words of Bishop William A. Hughes, of the American bishops' Committee on Priestly Life and Ministry, that "the vast majority of Catholic people are unhappy with the quality of Sunday preaching." Perhaps that is one factor in the alarming statistic published by the Catholic Evangelization Center in 1982 that the number of non-practicing Catholics tripled during the 1970s.

Of course, some might want to take refuge in the historical fact that poor preaching is nothing new in the Church. Blessed Humbert of Romans, for example, who lived from c. 1200 to 1277, A.D., wrote while he was fifth Master General of the Order of Preachers:

> There are only a few good preachers. In the primitive Church there were few preachers, but they were so good that they converted the whole world. Now there are preachers too many to count, but they achieve little. (*Treatise on the Formation of Preachers*, VII, 79.)

Preaching was also poor in the early days of the Church in the United States. James Hennesey, S.J., in his history, *American Catholics*, quotes John Carroll, Superior of the Mission in the Thirteen Colonies of the United States of North America, (later first bishop of Baltimore) in the late eighteenth century as being critical of the quality of preaching in the Catholic congregations he visited.

A hundred years later, evidently things had not improved. In his brief historical monograph, *Catholic Sunday Preaching: The American Guidelines, 1791-1975*, Robert F. McNamara cites some of the common faults from the pulpit endured by Catholics in the nineteenth century: "long-windedness, irrelevance, crudity, insensitivity to non-

Catholic listeners, unpreparedness, billingsgate, making a poor mouth, and violating professional confidences." (p. 19)

In spite of the long-standing nature and seriousness of the problem, the American bishops, as they have so frequently done in the past through synodal legislation, are once again moving to solutions. In 1982 they issued a pastoral document on preaching, *Fulfilled in Your Hearing: The Homily in the Sunday Assembly*. The first reason they give for the issuance of the pastoral at this time is: "the conclusions of numerous surveys indicating the questionable quality of preaching and homily preparation often experienced in Catholic churches."

The Word of God Institute has been dedicated to contributing to the movement for better preaching in the Roman Catholic Church in the United States since 1972. It was founded as a result of the First National Congress on the Word of God, celebrated at the National Shrine of the Immaculate Conception, Washington, D.C., to channel the creative energies generated by the Holy Spirit during that Congress into all aspects of the Church's life.

The Institute consists of an Episcopal Advisory Board, Board of Councilors, Associates and skilled resource persons. Working closely together, they enable the Institute to offer theological perspective, professional competence and evangelical enthusiasm to the ministry of preaching. The Word of God Institute exists to help bishops, priests, laity — indeed all preachers — become more firmly rooted in the Word of God and so more effective preachers and witnesses to the life-giving Gospel of Jesus Christ.

Five years after its founding, the Word of God Institute sponsored the First National Congress on Evangelization in St. Paul-Minneapolis. Bishops, priests, deacons, religious and laity came together in faith and in the Holy Spirit to explore how the Church could make its proclamation of the Gospel more fruitful.

The hopes of Pope Paul VI were expressed in a letter to the Congress:

His Holiness ... looks forward to seeing sound programs in evangelization being fostered, through the grace
of God, as a concrete result of the Congress. (Letter from
Cardinal Villot.)

Many such programs did come about nationally and locally
in the life of the Church because of the rich blessings of the
Holy Spirit on the Congress on Evangelization.

All of this brings us to the National Ecumenical
Scriptural-Theological Symposium on Preaching at Emory
University, whence these chapters. The Symposium was
intended as a contribution to the revitalization of preaching
in our own day by the Word of God Institute in joint
sponsorship with the Southern Dominican Province of St.
Martin de Porres.

Certainly, as the early paragraphs of this introduction
have indicated, there is no single or simple answer to the
many complex problems of preaching from a Church
marked by diversity to a world wounded by division. Nevertheless, the essays in this book, written by ten of the most
brilliant minds in the Christian Churches today can be
helpful to the thoughtful and responsive reader, whether
preacher or listener. The writers concern themselves with
issues that go to the very core of the preaching ministry; they
treat of those aspects which are perennially normative for
fruitful preaching.

Walter J. Burghardt links the proclamation of the word
of God from the pulpit to the assimilation of the word of
God in the study through the preacher's experience of God,
His people, and His works.

Raymond E. Brown, with his expected clarity of vision
and development uses the critical tools of the Scripture
scholar to draw out the implications of the preaching done
in the Acts of the Apostles for our own day. He thus
provides a basic scriptural norm for contemporary praxis.

Edward K. Braxton, carefully differentiating the kinds of
conversion that human beings undergo in life, relates the
preaching of the Gospel to the life of faith in individuals and
the community.

William J. Hill situates the act of preaching in the total theological process in order to arrive at a more intimate conjunction of thinking about God and proclaiming Him.

And finally, Leander E. Keck explores in detail Paul's understanding of divine wisdom as found in the First Letter to the Corinthians which remains normative for Christian preaching today.

Each essay is commented upon by an outstanding Church leader to both clarify the original paper and to draw out explicitly what was only implied.

Certain common themes emerge from these essays which can be of immediate practical help to the preacher. First, it is essential that preachers employ the tools of modern biblical criticism which is not only tolerated but endorsed by the Church and which the Church expects its preachers to use as a guide in the interpretation of Scripture in the contemporary Church.

Secondly, there is the need on the part of the preacher to rethink, to re-interpret old truths in the light of the contemporary situation by the exercise of a disciplined theological methodolgy.

Thirdly, preaching depends on the "experience" of both God and listener, on the part of the preacher. This means that more is required than abstract knowledge of universal truths by the intellect alone. Rather, the preacher needs to know the singular in all of its unique particularity as well. This kind of experiential knowledge is shaped by the senses and the emotions; it is time and place-conditioned, related to feelings of the heart as well as understanding by the mind. It makes possible the statement: "I do not just know about Jesus; I know Jesus Himself as a person."

At the same time, there seems to be a reaction against the kind of preaching directed solely to the individual. While insisting upon the experiential, preaching occurs always in an ecclesial context. That is, preaching at its most efficacious level is formative of Christian community as well as having its origins in Christian community.

Finally, another theme common to these essays is the utter gratuity of God's favor towards us. It is a favor which evokes a response on our part and which finds a fullness of expression in the Cross and Resurrection.

In order for preaching to be effective, to change hearts and minds, to form community, to bear fruit in terms of human holiness, in short, in order to communicate the Gospel message, the preacher needs to undertake the life-long, disciplined and graced task of synthesizing these interrelated elements into a cohesive expression of living faith whch is the act of preaching.

The Word of God Institute, its Episcopal Advisory Board, Councilors and Staff are deeply grateful to all who made the Symposium the exciting experience of renewal it was: to our presenters and respondents, certainly; but also, to our patrons and benefactors; and especially, to those dedicated men and women who responded so generously to our invitation and gave themselves so whole-heartedly to the demanding exploration of the Symposium sessions.

It is our prayer that, under the inspiration of the Holy Spirit, this volume may be a significant help to preachers of the Gospel as they fulfill the solemn charge of the Second Letter to Timothy:

> Before God and before Christ Jesus who is to be judge of the living and the dead, I put this duty to you, in the name of his appearing and his kingdom, proclaim the message and welcome or unwelcome, insist on it.

From Study To Proclamation
Walter J. Burghardt, S.J.

Response
Elisabeth Schüssler Fiorenza

From Study To Proclamation
Walter J. Burghardt, S.J.

Long centuries ago, a student in a select school looked
longingly at his teacher and begged him: "Teach us how to
pray" (Lk 11:1). Because that particular teacher was filled
with the Holy Spirit, and perhaps because his human intelligence was uniquely wed to divine Wisdom, he did teach the
class how to pray: "When you pray, say..." (v. 2).

For decades, seminarians beyond counting have looked
longingly at their professors and begged them: "Teach us
how to preach." And the masters in theology, presumably
enlightened by the self-same Spirit, have failed to serve up a
satisfying "When you preach, preach like this...." Some
have coldly rejected the request as foreign to their function,
the burden of homiletics. Others have desperately tagged
practical applications onto theological theses: a paragraph
of kitchen Christology; an appendix in ecclesiology on the
family as a little church; and so on weakly into the night.
The theologian was not a preacher, and the homiletics
professor was rarely a theologian. And so the new priest has
departed the seminary with a theology that often bored him,
and a course in homiletics that stressed technique, know-
how, "how to." Wired for sound, not fired for proclamation.

In consequence, we continue to reap the plaintive protests
of our parishioners: Why have so many priests so little to
say? Aren't you "turned on" by this God you've studied so

25

long at our expense? Whatever happened to you fellows when you "left the world"?

Less passionately phrased, the problem might read: How do you move effectively from classroom to pulpit, from study to proclamation? There is no instant answer, no infallible injection, no universal lesson. The homily that "sends" worshipers to the vaults of St. Patrick's Cathedral may fall flat on the grass of a rude chapel in Micronesia. No preaching pattern works for the Curé d'Ars *and* Norman Vincent Peale. Even you and I will preach differently from the same pulpit, to the same people. Your "style" is not my "style."

It is not my task, therefore, to write your homily, not my task to set before you, in living color, "the very model of a modern major" homilist.[1] I shall attempt something far less arrogant and far more basic, something I have come to see with increasing intensity in the twilight of my life. It is my contention that between study and proclamation there is frequently a missing link. That link is experience: experience of God, experience of God's people, experience of God's wonderful works. And that link spells the difference between the journeyman and the master. To make this thesis perceptible and palatable, let me unfold it in three stages, under three rubrics: (1) study, (2) experience, (3) proclamation.

I

First, study. By "study" I mean a searching for knowledge, a searching that is organized, disciplined, methodical. It might take a solid semester or a single hour. It might be a complete course in Christology or a serious "Saturday Night Live," with Padre Sarducci feverishly plundering

---

[1]The reference is to a line in the Gilbert and Sullivan operetta *The Pirates of Penzance* (1879): "the very model of a modern major general."

Raymond Brown on Jesus' enigmatic words to Pilate, "*You*
say I am a king" (Jn 18:37).[2] In any event, it is a deliberate
effort to learn something in student style.

Now my four decades of preaching tell me that very little
I've studied is impertinent to preaching. From anthropology to zoology, whatever you learn about God's creation is
potential grist for your homiletic mill. Not that you study
every subject, or any subject, simply to see how you can
apply it to the pulpit. Such study, such "despoiling of the
Egyptians,"[3] not only does violence to the autonomy of a
science; it risks turning superficial, and it contributes little
or nothing to your constant conversion. My point is, whatever you study can offer fresh insight into God's awesome
activity in the story of salvation. I recall here what the
perceptive Lutheran theologian Joseph Sittler found want-
ing in Vatican II's Constitution on the Church in the Modern World:

> The doctrine of grace remains trapped within the rubric
> of redemption, while at the same time the joys, hopes,
> griefs and anxieties that evoke the document are most
> sharply delineated under the rubric of creation.... What
> is required is nothing short of a doctrine of grace elabo-
> rated as fully under the article of God the Creator as a
> doctrine of grace has been historically developed under
> the article of God the Redeemer.[4]

[2] A reference to a popular TV show.

[3] A favorite early Christian expression for appropriating "pagan truth" in the
interests of the faith: Whatever there is of truth among you really belongs to us.

[4] Joseph Sittler, "A Protestant Point of View," in John H. Miller, C.S.C., ed.,
Vatican II: An Interfaith Appraisal (Notre Dame: University of Notre Dame,
c1966) 426. In a later article ("Ecological Commitment as Theological Responsibility," *Idoc*, Sept. 12, 1970, 75-85) Sittler insisted that our basic ecological error is
that we Christians have separated creation and redemption. The reason why we
can worship nature in Vermont and at the same time manipulate nature in New
York is because, in our view, the redemption wrought by Christ leaves untouched
the creation wrought by God. And once we wrench redemption from creation,
once we put nature out there and grace in here, as long as we omit from our
theology of grace the transaction of man and woman with nature, it is irrelevant to
Christians whether we reverence the earth or ravish it.

Our Catholic tradition tends to draw too hard and fast a line between nature and grace, between the secular and the sacred. The peril of too sharp a distinction is that nature and the secular can be misprized and despised. No, God's salvific story is everywhere to hear and discern: not only in "the heavens" that "are telling the glory of God" (Ps 19:1) but all over our planet, from the ovum and sperm that join to shape a child to the Atari and the atom. The divine milieu, as Teilhard de Chardin saw, is not only the mystical body of Christ; it is the cosmic body of Christ. The matter of your homily, therefore, is literally without limit.

But lest this essay be limitless, I focus on two areas of study particularly pertinent for the preacher. The first is Scripture — Old Testament and New. No need to argue its peerless importance; give ear to Vatican II:

> Like the Christian religion itself, all the preaching of the Church must needs be nourished and governed by Sacred Scripture. In the sacred books, you see, the Father who is in heaven comes to meet His children with extraordinary love and speaks with them. So remarkable is its power and force that the word of God abides as the support and energy of the Church, the strength of faith for the Church's children, the food of the soul, the pure and perennial source of spiritual life.[5]

If that is true, if for those striking reasons all our preaching should find its direction and its sustenance in Scripture, a twin challenge confronts us. One facet is general, the other quite specific. On broad lines, my homily should be recognizably biblical. For all my radiant twentieth-century rhetoric, I must confess that there is an incomparable power, an unrivaled richness, in the sheer text of Scripture. Why? Raymond Brown has put the reason pithily: "In the Bible God communicates Himself to the extraordinary extent that one can say that there is something 'of God' in the

---

[5]Constitution on Divine Revelation, no. 21.

words. All other works, patristic, Thomistic, and ecclesias-
tic, are words *about* God; only the Bible is the word *of*
God."[6] And the scriptural symbols, from the covenant
through the kingdom to the cross, are matchless for their
capacity to evoke a religious response.

But if I am to mediate the unique power of God's word to
others, the Bible cannot remain a mere reference book, a
handy volume of quotations for all occasions. Scripture
must be the air I breathe. I must develop a love for God's
word that reflects the vivid advice of St. Jerome: "When
your head droops at night, let a page of Scripture pillow it."[7]
Only so will *my* words too burn with Isaian fire; only so will
the ancient symbols come alive on my lips; only so will the
"good news" come across to the faithful as news indeed, and
as very, very good.

This is highly important, this immersion in the Bible like
an embryo in amniotic fluid. But by itself it is not enough;
something more specific must supplement it. After all, God
is not simply "talking." He is saying something: "Thus says
the Lord." "Amen, amen, I say to you." To recapture what
that is calls for disciplined study. What did the Lord actually
mean when He proclaimed through Jeremiah: "This is the
covenant which I will make with the house of Israel after
those days . . .: I will put my law within them, and I will write
it upon their hearts; and I will be their God, and they shall be
my people" (Jer 31:33)? Not my personal preference for
beatitudes, but why Matthew and Luke are so different; why
Luke has Jesus talking about real poverty, Matthew poverty
in spirit. How you reconcile the radical Jesus on riches with
the moderate Jesus: the Jesus for whom wealth is "totally
linked with evil"[8] and the Jesus who counsels a prudent use

---

[6]Raymond E. Brown, S.S., "'And the Lord Said'? Biblical Reflections on
Scripture as the Word of God," *Theological Studies* 42 (1981) 3-19, at 18. The
whole article should be read for its careful effort to grasp the meaning of Scripture
as *God's* word.

[7]Jerome, *Letter 22*, 17.

[8]So Josef Schmid, *The Gospel According to Mark* (Regensburg New Testament;
Staten Island, N.Y.: Alba [1968]) 194.

of possessions; the Jesus who tells some people to give it all away and the Jesus who advises others to share what they have; the Jesus who forces you to choose between money and God, and the Jesus who loves a rich man who keeps both his wealth and God's commandments.

I am not suggesting that to be an effective preacher you must become a professional exegete. I am not identifying what a biblical text meant to its human author *then* with what God may be saying to you through the text *now*. I am even prepared to grant, with Gadamer and contemporary philosophical hermeneutics, that a so-called "classical" text, be it the Bible or a score of Chopin, "has a fulness of meaning which by its very nature can never be exhausted," that "the meaning mediated by the [classical] text actually exceeds the conscious intention of the author," that the reader's understanding can help constitute the meaning of the text, "as the interpretation of the artist is constitutive of the music."[9] If that is true, then the ordinary Christian, operating within the understanding of the faith community and out of his or her life experience, can grasp what the text is basically saying. "Just as one need not be a professional musician to enjoy a symphony, or a literary critic to enjoy *Moby Dick*, one need not be a professional exegete to understand the Gospel of Luke."[10]

And still you dare not disregard scholarly exegesis. Sandra Schneiders has phrased it tellingly, in the context of philosophical hermeneutics:

> The advantage of the exegete is analogous to that of the professional musician. Obviously, one who can play Chopin can, other things being equal, enjoy Chopin more deeply than the musically uneducated but appreciative listener. Even more importantly, unless *someone* can play Chopin, the ordinary person will never have the

[9]Sandra M. Schneiders, I.H.M., "Faith, Hermeneutics, and the Literal Sense of Scripture," *Theological Studies* 39 (1978) 719-36, at 731 and 732. See H.G. Gadamer, *Truth and Method* (New York: Seabury, 1975) esp. 235-341.

[10]Schneiders, "Faith" 733.

chance to appreciate his music.... Through the work of exegesis the text becomes more available and more understandable, just as through the playing of the musician the music becomes more available and more enjoyable.[11]

If you are to preach the word of God effectively today, a double don't is in order: (1) Don't bypass the exegete. (2) Don't parrot the exegete. The paradox is startling: You are more likely to grasp what God's word says today if you have mastered what God's word meant yesterday.

The second area of study particularly pertinent for the preacher is theology. Simply because theology is the Church's ceaseless struggle to understand God's word and to express it. It is theology's privilege and burden to search out *where* God has spoken, where God speaks: from the burning bush in Midian to the gas ovens in Auschwitz, from the word that was creation to the Word that was made flesh, from the Church gathered in council to the skin-and-bones dying that defecate at Calcutta's curbstones, from the Book that somehow reveals the heart of God to the trace of God on the face of humanity.

It is theology's task to uncover and interpret *what* God has said, what God says now. It is to theologians of the past 1800 years — from Irenaeus to Rahner — that you owe your deeper understanding of so many love-laden mysteries. I mean, who *Christ* is: what it means to be divine and what it means to be human — both in the one unique package. What the *Church* is: not only or primarily the hierarchy, but the whole interpersonal community united to the Father and to one another through Christ in the Spirit. What *grace* means: the vast, deep realm that is the relationship between a triune God and the human person. What it means to say that God has revealed Himself to us in His dying-rising Son, that God channels His life to us in the sacraments, that Christ is really present in the Eucharist, that death is not the close of life but its glorious continuance days without end.

It is not theology you preach; for the pulpit is not a classroom. But without theology you risk preaching platitudes (Remember Mayor Daley's "Chicago must rise to higher and higher platitudes"?). Our homilies are rarely heretical. They fail rather because they are stale and flat, vapid and insipid, dreadfully dry and boringly barren. One reason? They are not pregnant with the inexhaustible riches that is Christ; they have so little substance, so little sap to slake the parched spirit.

II

Serious study, therefore, is important for the preacher. Exegesis and theology exist because each word God speaks is at once mysterious and open-ended, never totally understood. Exegetes and theologians help you to take that word from wherever it is spoken, wrestle with it, feel its fire, and fling it out to live people with new life, fresh flame.

But sheer study is not enough. To preach effectively, to speak God's word as Isaiah and Paul, it is not enough to know *about* God; I must know God. In half a century, I have learned a good deal about God. With Aquinas, I have learned that God is Immovable Mover, Uncaused Cause, Necessary Being, Absolute Perfection, Supreme End. With Paul, I have risen from "the things that have been made" to God's "invisible nature," to "His eternal power and deity" (Rom 1:20). With John, I believe "God so loved the world that He gave His only Son" (Jn 3:16), gave him to a crucifying death that I might have life. I resonate to Joseph Mary Plunkett when he sees Christ's "blood upon the rose,/ And in the stars the glory of his eyes./ His body gleams amid eternal snows,/ His tears fall from the skies."[12] I thrill when I read in Gerard Manley Hopkins that I can find God in man and woman, that "Christ plays in ten thousand places,/

---

[12] Joseph Mary Plunkett, "I See His Blood upon the Rose," in Thomas Walsh, ed., *The Catholic Anthology: The World's Great Catholic Poetry* (rev. ed.; New York: Macmillan, 1947) 428.

Lovely in limbs, and lovely in eyes not his/ To the Father through the features of men's faces."[13]

But believe me, this is not enough. From my own checkered past, I urge on all preachers a burning, humbling question: For all you know *about* God, do you really know God? Several years ago Karl Rahner fashioned a moving essay in the form of a letter from Ignatius Loyola to a modern Jesuit. A significant segment of the letter has to do with Ignatius' experience of God. Here simply some excerpts:

> I was convinced that first, tentatively, during my illness in Loyola and then, decisively, during my time as a hermit in Manresa I had a direct encounter with God. This was the experience I longed to communicate to others.... I am not going to talk of forms and visions, symbols, voices, tears and such things. All I say is I knew God, nameless and unfathomable, silent and yet near, bestowing himself upon me in his Trinity. I knew God beyond all concrete imaginings. I knew him clearly in such nearness and grace as is impossible to confound or mistake....
>
> God himself: I knew God himself, not simply human words describing him.... This experience is grace indeed and basically there is no one to whom it is refused.... When I say that it is as possible to encounter God in your age as in mine, I mean God really and truly, the God of incomprehensibility, the ineffable mystery, the darkness which only becomes eternal light for the man who allows himself to be swallowed up by it unconditionally. But it is precisely this God, he and none other, whom I personally experienced as the God who comes down to us, who comes close to us, the God in whose incomprehensible fire we are not, in fact, burnt away but become ourselves and of eternal value. The ineffable God promises himself to us; and in this promise of his ineffa-

---

[13]Gerard Manley Hopkins, "As kingfishers catch fire...," in W. H. Gardner and N. H. MacKenzie, eds., *The Poems of Gerard Manley Hopkins* (4th ed.; London: Oxford University, 1975) 90.

bility we become, we live, we are loved and we are of eternal value; through him, if we allow ourselves to be taken up by him, we are not destroyed but given to ourselves truly for the first time.[14]

Can you say that, like Ignatius, you have truly encountered the living and true God? Can you say that you know God Himself, not simply human words that describe Him? If you cannot, I dare not conclude that you are an unproductive preacher; for the same God who "is able from these stones to raise up children to Abraham" (Mt 3:9) can use the most sere of sermons to move the obdurate heart. But I do say that if you know only a theology of God, not the God of theology, you will not be the preacher our world desperately needs.

To know God, it is not enough to memorize Mark, translate Trent, ransack Rahner. The Father, His Christ, their Spirit — these must come through to you as real persons, real as the flesh-and-blood man or woman next to you. Your personal experience of God, how God speaks to you, this is not mine to define. It may be the thunder of Sinai (Exod 19:19) or the "still small voice" on Horeb (1 Kgs 19:12). It may be the theophany to a rebellious Job, where God transpires not to defend His wisdom but to stress His mystery. It may be Francis stigmatized on Alvernia or Augustine and Monica enravished at Ostia. It may be John of the Cross's ascent of Carmel or Ignatius' illumination at the Cardoner.

More likely, your encounter with God will mean that you are increasingly sensitive to four phenomenological aspects of your relationship to God in Christ.[15] (1) You will find yourself absorbed by a *living* presence, a divine activity more real than your physical surroundings. (2) You will be aware of a *holy* presence that fills you with awe and fear, the

---

[14]Karl Rahner, S.J., and Paul Imhof, S.J., *Ignatius of Loyola* (New York: Collins, c1978) 11, 12, 13, 17.

[15]The rest of this paragraph is indebted to Pierre Fransen, "Towards a Psychology of Divine Grace," *Cross Currents* 8 (1958) 229-30.

while it warms and draws you — what Mouroux called "a kind of rhythm between hope and fear, each mutually supporting and generating the other."[16] (3) You will know an inexpressible *loneliness*; for in the presence of Love you will still be far from Love, agonizingly aware that to find yourself you must lose yourself, to grasp God you must risk all. (4) Even within sorrow you will sense a profound *joy*, strong and unshakable, a joy that refuses to be imprisoned, must burst forth to be shared with others.

In the last analysis, as the fourth-century theologian and mystic Gregory of Nyssa saw so perceptively, there is only one way to know God, and that is to be like Him, to get to be in His image. And so

> the knowledge of God to which [Gregory] gives preference in his thinking is that of participation in His virtues, in His holiness — that knowledge which is essentially union.... And how participate in that holiness of God? By following Him through faith, eyes closed, wherever He leads; by opening one's heart always to a further and deeper submissiveness; by divesting oneself of every favor already received through unceasing yearning for what is always beyond; in a word, by the ecstasy which is a going out of oneself....[17]

Our people are hungry for preachers who, like Magdalene, have seen the risen Lord. My darkest moments in homiletics are not when my theology is porous. My darkest moments are when I have ceased to pray — when the familiar phrases fall trippingly from my pen and tongue but it is all rote, prepackaged, with the life-giving juices dried up. My preaching is least effective when I experience nothing — neither God's presence nor His absence.

---

[16]Jean Mouroux, *The Christian Experience: An Introduction to a Theology* (New York: Sheed and Ward, 1954) 38.

[17]This summary of Gregory stems from Roger Leys, *L'Image de Dieu chez Grégoire de Nysse* (Brussels: L'Edition Universelle, 1951) 139-40.

Not unexpectedly, the same problem surges in regard of God's images on earth. My homiletic experience cries aloud that Christian anthropology is not enough. Important indeed, but insufficient. The preacher our people desperately need not only knows *about* man and woman. Our people need preachers who live what Aquinas put so acutely: "There are two ways of desiring knowledge. One way is to desire it as a perfection of one's self; and that is the way philosophers desire it. The other way is to desire it not [merely] as a perfection of one's self, but because through this knowledge the one we love becomes present to us; and that is the way saints desire it."

This is not to denigrate anthropology. I am simply saying that the most profound knowledge is in peril of staying sterile unless it is charged with love. My knowledge of the human condition is Christian and salvific, my insight into man and woman will find effective expression, if it touches me to the other, to the countless men and women whose days are faithless or hopeless or loveless.

The paradox is, the flow is not one way. Here is reciprocal causality, a two-way street. If knowledge leads to love, love deepens knowledge. It has taken me a lifetime to learn that love lavished on others is not time stolen from theology, from anthropology, from homiletics. Please God, you will learn, not so much from reading as from loving, how "Christ plays in ten thousand places...through the features of men's faces."

Something similar can be said about the rest of God's creation. It is not enough for you to plumb its secrets; you should experience the subhuman as sacred. Everything that exists, from ocean floor to outer space, is precious because it reflects the God whose whole being is summed up in a monosyllable: He *is*. And everything that lives, from the simple amoeba through a field of wheat to the sulphur-bottom whale, is more precious still, because it images the God who *is* Life. This breath-taking trace of God throughout His universe is not yours simply to know, to recognize, to analyze. To preach persuasively, you had better love it!

Perhaps what I have said so far can be summed up neatly. A solid sermon presupposes serious study, if only because the word you preach is not so much your word as God's word; and God's word is a challenge not only to your piety but to your intelligence. But sheer study is insufficient; for to study is, in large measure, to recapture the ideas and insights, the discoveries and experiences of others. If you are to do more than parrot the exegete and theologian, if you are to touch God's living word to a living people, you have to hear that word with your own ears, see the risen Christ with your own eyes, experience for yourself the Lord God and the loving work of His hands.

Let me point up and conclude this segment on experience with a story I have borrowed from Henri Nouwen:

One day a young fugitive, trying to hide himself from the enemy, entered a small village. The people were kind to him and offered him a place to stay. But when the soldiers who sought the fugitive asked where he was hiding, everyone became very fearful. The soldiers threatened to burn the village and kill every man in it unless the young man were handed over to them before dawn. The people went to the minister and asked him what to do. The minister, torn between handing over the boy to the enemy or having his people killed, withdrew to his room and read his Bible, hoping to find an answer before dawn. After many hours, in the early morning his eyes fell on these words: "It is better that one man dies than that the whole people be lost."

Then the minister closed the Bible, called the soldiers, and told them where the boy was hidden. And after the soldiers led the fugitive away to be killed, there was a feast in the village because the minister had saved the lives of the people. But the minister did not celebrate. Overcome with a deep sadness, he remained in his room. That night an angel came to him and asked, "What have you done?" He said: "I handed over the fugitive to the enemy." Then the angel said: "But don't you know that you have handed over the Messiah?" "How could I know?" the minister replied anxiously. Then the angel said: "If, instead of reading your Bible, you

had visited this young man just once and looked into his eyes, you would have known."[18]

III

Study impregnated with experience — a powerful preparation for preaching. But as yet I do not have an actual sermon or homily; the word I shall personally proclaim has not taken specific shape. How shape it? No single system ensures success for all. Still, for what it is worth, let me sketch my own *modus operandi*. Here I recapture a real-life situation: the second Sunday of Advent 1982, cycle C, a homily I was asked to deliver at the National Shrine of the Immaculate Conception in Washington, D.C.

Stage 1: What shall I talk about? This is the mulling stage, the search for a subject, the general topic. It has to focus on Advent, of course. But what approach to Advent? I could fashion my homily directly from the liturgical readings (Bar 5:1-9; Phil 1:4-6, 8-11; Lk 3:1-6), but something else intrigues me more. I recall, from a lecture by Raymond Brown, that three persons dominate the Advent liturgy —three persons who prepare in different ways for the coming of the Savior: Isaiah, John the Baptist, Mary. And the feast of the Immaculate Conception is almost upon us — three days away. I have my topic: Advent with Mary.

Stage 2: How, in point of fact, do Advent and Mary link up? This calls for study in two areas: What is the Advent liturgy all about, and how does Mary fit into it? Advent, I find, is a period of expectation; we are waiting. For what? We focus on two events. We put ourselves back into the situation of an expectant people, on tiptoe for the first coming of the Messiah; and we rekindle our expectation of his final coming. Baruch waits for the first coming, Paul for the final.

---

[18] Henri J. M. Nouwen, *The Wounded Healer: Ministry in Contemporary Society* (Garden City, N.Y.: Doubleday, 1972) 25-26. This is apparently only one version of a very ancient story.

And what of Mary? As I search the Scriptures and can-
vass the commentaries, I conclude that Mary and Advent fit
together strikingly. Not primarily because we celebrate
Mary's birthday on September 8, subtract nine months, and
celebrate her conception on December 8. Mary is an Advent
figure because she reveals more remarkably than anyone
else how the Christian should wait for Christ. First, the way
she waited for Christ's *first* coming. Not only like every
other Jew waiting for the Promised One. She waited uniquely, as no other in history: He for whom she was waiting was
nestling within her, in her flesh. She was waiting only to see
his face and to offer him to the world. Second, the way Mary
waited for Christ's *second* coming. In a word, she was his
disciple — the very model of what discipleship means. "My
mother and my brothers, they are the ones who listen to the
word of God and act on it" (Lk 8:21). That, at its best, is
Mary: she who hears God's word and does it. Such was
Mary at the Gospel's beginning; such was she throughout
her life (check this theme in Luke); such was she beneath the
cross; such was she after the ascension of her Son, waiting
with the Eleven for the descent of the Spirit.

Stage 3: How organize all this? It seems to suggest three
points, three questions. The first two stem naturally from
my study: (1) What is the Advent liturgy all about? Expectant waiting for Christ. (2) How does Mary fit into Advent?
History's most remarkable model of waiting: She listened to
the word of God and acted on it. But a third question
challenges not my study but my experience: What does
Mary say to us these Advent weeks? She shows us how to
wait for Christ. Not only for his second coming, "with great
power and glory" (Mk 13:26); for his constant coming each
day, in poverty and powerlessness that make his crib look
like a castle. This is not pious poetry; it is the word of God.
Jesus comes to us in the hungry and thirsty, in the stranger
and the naked, in the sick and the shackled (cf. Mt 25:35-40).
The hungers of the human family cry out to us: hunger for
bread, for justice and peace, for understanding and love
—hunger for God. Their cry is not only a human cry; God is
speaking to us. We are Jesus' disciples, in the image of

Mary, only if we listen to that anguished word and act on it, as God gives us to act.

Stage 4: I develop each point in detail, compose in organized fashion, order my ideas with rigor and vigor. Here clarity, for all its importance, is not enough. A homily is not a catechism, not a theology text, not a curial rescript; it calls for a religious response. And so I struggle with language, wrestle with words; Webster's Unabridged is my second bible. I pause to read Shakespeare aloud, Gerard Manley Hopkins, T. S. Eliot, Tennessee Williams. I listen to Beethoven's *Ninth Symphony* or Barber's *Adagio*, a ballet like *Swan Lake* or a dash of country music. For the bare message can be deadeningly dull; it must come alive, take wing. To play on the human heart, my words must leap and dance, quiver and shiver, burn and cool. That is why, when I speak to my Advent people about the hungers of the human family, I move briskly from abstractions to "the living skeletons in Mother Teresa's Calcutta and the downtrodden in D.C., the bombed-out in Lebanon and the MX in Wyoming, the slums in El Salvador and the pimps and prostitutes in Times Square, the schizoid psyches in St. Elizabeth's and the lonely old on your street."

But for my words to come alive, *I* must come alive. Which drives me back, time and again, not to study but to experience: How do I touch God in love, feel the scars of His people, trace His face in sky and earth?

Stage 5: When I think I've finished, I work through every sentence of the homily with a very fine comb. I don't need this much on Isaiah, that extra phrase on John the Baptist. A purple patch here, a bit too subtle there. Block that metaphor, excise that hackneyed expression, lessen the alliteration. Not a single needless word.

I have mapped out one man's movement from study through experience to proclamation. If it strikes you as onerous and time-consuming, I shall not quarrel with you; it takes me sixty or seventy hours to shape a fifteen-minute homily. But, I assure you, the results outstrip the price: for your people, time and again fresh insight into the mind of

Christ, often a burning yearning to listen to the Lord and say yes; for yourself, a continuing education, ever-new experience of the risen Christ, constant conversion. Yes, conversion; for you will soon discover that in the first instance you are preaching to yourself. The people will listen more eagerly, to the Lord and His preacher, if the preacher has seen the Lord's face.

Let me leave you with a comforting thought — comforting and unexpectedly practical. There is hardly an experience in your day that is not grist for your proclamation. I do not mean that you carry a notebook, jot down every single thing that passes for real. I do mean that everything you see, hear, touch, taste, and smell is part of your human and Christian experience, can therefore shape the word you preach and the way you preach it. *Chariots of Fire, On Golden Pond,* and *E.T.*; the photo of Mother Teresa cradling a naked retarded child in West Beirut; the Op. Ed. page and the debate on nuclear morality; the taste of canneloni and the cool breeze caressing your cheek; thousands of Cambodian refugees ravaged by tuberculosis, dysentery, malaria; the latest in song hits and the plaints of your people; the touch of a hand, the feel of a flower, the look of love in another's eyes; the Christ who each day pillows himself in your palm and graces your body. These experiences and a thousand more combine to fashion the person you are. Let them fashion your homily as well. In this way your life and your preaching will sing the joyous eucharist of the poet e. e. cummings:

> i thank You God for most this amazing
> day: for the leaping greenly spirits of trees
> and a blue true dream of sky; and for everything
> which is natural which is infinite which is yes
>
> (i who have died am alive again today,
> and this is the sun's birthday; this is the birth
> day of life and of love and wings: and of the gay
> great happening illimitably earth)

how should tasting touching hearing seeing
breathing any — lifted from the no
of all nothing — human merely being
doubt unimaginable You?

(now the ears of my ears awake and
now the eyes of my eyes are opened)[19]

This, at bottom, is your homily: thanksgiving for most this amazing day, for everything which is natural, for everything which is infinite, for everything which is yes. So be it!

---

[19]e. e. cummings, Poem 95 in *100 Poems*.

Response
Elisabeth Schüssler Fiorenza

Professor Burghardt has very eloquently outlined how the homilist moves from study to proclamation. He has stressed the necessity for careful study of Scripture and theology. He has emphasized the importance of the preacher's experience of God, "the Father and His Christ," and finally he has outlined the five stages of "one man's movement from study through experience to proclamation." The argument of the paper is insightful, formulated with great care, and well balanced. I envy his skill as "a weaver of words."

We are all in debt to Father Burghardt for his stimulating presentation. It goes without saying that his constructive proposals are both suggestive and provocative and I have no serious disagreement to register. In my response I should therefore like to underline his emphasis on experience and on the study of Holy Scripture by singling out three points or areas where I would want to complement his suggestions and at the same time to offer a somewhat different perspective on the interrelationship between experience, study and proclamation. Such a different perspective comes from my expertise not as a homilist but as a Scripture scholar and a feminist theologian. The three areas I wish to focus on are: (1) the interpretation of present experience not only of the

homilist but of all the people of God, (2) the interpretation
of past experiences of the people of God in Scripture, and
(3) the move from experience to proclamation.

I. Interpretation of Present Experiences of All the People of God

Dr. Burghardt addresses foremost the homilist and his
God-experience. His movement from study to experience to
proclamation entails three major components: the first is
study, the third and last is proclamation. The interlocking
link in his proposal is experience. Experience is so to speak
the missing link between study and proclamation. How does
Father Burghardt understand experience? It is defined as
the "experience of God, the experience of God's people and
the experience of God's wonderful works." God's people are
not the subject of experience but are here conceived of as a
part of the object of the homilist's experience. Moreover he
maintains that in order to preach the homilist must not just
know something *about* God. Experience is specified as the
homilist's experience *of* God and it is this almost mystical
experience of God that provides the link between study and
proclamation. The homilist's experience is paradigmatic for
Christian God-experience today.

Yet some of the major insights of recent theology stem
from the application of the sociology of knowledge to theology. Raw experience or even common experience does not
exist, but what exists are particular and individual experiences. All human experience insofar as it is human experience is bound to particular historical situations, is bound to
specific cultural contexts, and is determined or at least
influenced by the individual's social status and professional
role in society and church. This social conditioning of experience holds true also for the human experience of God.
There is not an abstract common experience of God, but
human experience of God is a particular experience that
reflects and is shaped by its historical conditions in time and

space, in culture and gender socialization. It is for this reason that I think it is important to look at exprience not just as a link but also as a starting point of the movement from study to proclamation. The conditioning of experience poses the hermeneutical circle: where do we begin; how do we reflect upon our own experiences; how do we become conscious of our own presuppositions; how do we articulate our assumptions; how do we make explicit our institutional commitments?

My own critical starting point is not that of the homilist or the ordained cleric but that of the proverbial "woman in the pew," the silenced majority. Whereas the experience of God, and more and more also the study of Scripture and theology, is open to all persons who are religious and call themselves Christians — and not just to those who are called "religious" — this is not the case for proclamation. Whereas all the people of God — clergy and lay, men and women, rich and poor — can experience God's grace and presence in their lives, proclamation is limited in the Roman Catholic Church by law to celibate male clergy only. For all practical purposes women of the past and of the present have not preached and are in many Christian churches still excluded from *defining* the role of proclamation in terms of their own experience. In such an ecclesiastical situation the danger exists that the homily will not articulate the experience of God as the rich and pluriform experience of God's people, but that the male preacher will articulate his own experience and will declare and proclaim his own particular experience as the experience of God *par excellence*. What is limited and particular to his experience will be proclaimed as universal and paradigmatic for everyone. I would, therefore, suggest that in such a restrictive ecclesial situation the homilist has not just the function to articulate his own experience of God as a very particular experience but must also seek to articulate publicly the learning processes and the experiences of the people of God as well, since they are for the most part excluded from public proclamation. In order to be able to do so the homilist must become (1) self-critical, (2) attentive to the experiences of others not like himself, (3) seek the

involvement of those others in the task of preaching and proclamation and (4) develop dialogical modes and styles of preaching.

(1) Self-critical: To the extent that the homilist is aware of the hermeneutical circle he will become more and more self-critical. When he becomes aware of how experiences are embedded within a tradition, culture and society, the self-critical homilist will be on the alert not to substitute his own experience for that of the people of God, but rather seek to uncover the limitations of his own perspective and standpoint. Quite often I have heard sermons about the insecurity wrought among the faithful by Vatican II, where it was obvious that the problem was not that of the congregation but that of the preacher. I have listened, for instance, to sermons attacking the liberality of modern exegesis, especially, e.g., about the visit of the Magi, only to puzzle the audience, only to accomplish a moralist reduction of the text rather than a fuller development of its christological importance. I have patiently listened to diatribes against the desire for power, the lust after pride; sermons that may reflect male drives and sins but do not take into account the need of women to take control over their own lives or to be encouraged in their search for self-affirmation. I have listened to sermon after sermon denouncing our consumerist attitudes and self-serving wealth, sermons addressing the upper middle class members of the congregation but not those who struggle for economic survival. A homilist who has just returned suntanned from a vacation in Florida or Arizona is ill equipped to preach against the consumerism of a suburban housewife who has not had a vacation for years.

(2) Attentive to others' experience: One of the best ways of becoming self-critical is to listen carefully to the experiences of others rather than to project one's problems and fears into them. Liberation theology appeals to Scripture in pointing out that God can be found especially among the poor, the disadvantaged, the alienated, among those who do not belong. This does not mean that the poor and alienated are the objects of our charity and pastoral care so that they

receive from us out of the superabundance of our goods and wisdoms. But rather it means that we are to listen to their experiences of God, to their analysis of *how* our values, life-style, and pious self-security have led to and may have contributed to their exploitation and powerlessness, to their frustration and alienation, and may be the cause of their alienation from Christian faith and community. The homilist becomes self-critical when in such an attentive learning and listening process he becomes convinced that his own private experience is not the hermeneutical key to the experience of God, or that he, as ordained, is not hermeneutically privileged in regard to the Wisdom of Christ, but rather that this hermeneutical key is to be found with the poor, the disprivileged, and the alienated. Only by becoming attentive to the God-experiences of "others" who are not "like him," the homilist will become capable of relativizing his own stance and of connecting his own experience with the God-experience of others. Only then will he become capable of articulating the God-experiences of the people of God today in a fuller sense.

A recent experience may illustrate this. Just this Christmas I listened to a sermon in a Brooklyn parish in which the homilist complained that today we talk too much about "the brotherhood of men" but neglect to speak about "the Fatherhood of God." Obviously this preacher never listened to women who have become alienated from the Church and from God because of sexist language that erases them as subjects from the public discourse and liturgy of their church. He has never listened to the agony of women who need a whole week to recover their faith and hope after listening to a chauvinistic sermon on Sunday. I am sure that a great number of the women present did not notice or pay much attention to such androcentric preaching. Yet what about the ten or twenty percent who, like my daughter, are very conscious of the sin of sexism and no longer find themselves addressed by, or tolerant of, such male biased language and proclamation?

(3) Involvement of "others" in proclamation: Since no one single person can comprehend the multiform expe-

rience of the people of God or do justice to their legitimate religious needs, the homilist must seek to involve others in the move from experience to study to proclamation. Various models exist for such an involvement: Eduard Schweizer, a Swiss New Testament scholar and pastor, invites a group of parishioners to discuss and prepare the homily. Ernesto Cardenal has given us the scriptural dialogues of the peasants in Nicaragua. The *Gospel of Solentiname* teaches us how poor and alienated people can understand the meaning of the Gospel better than many highly trained middle-class exegetes do. This is not surprising because the New Testament Scriptures are rooted in the early Christian counter-cultural movement that was carried on for the most part by poor, alienated and disenfranchised people.

However, all partial involvement of the people of God in the preparation for proclamation does not suffice. The impoverishment of preaching today is not due to the lack of able preachers, but due to a structural clericalism which demands that one, single group of Christians — the ordained — articulate the richness and fullness of all Christians' God-experiences today. What is necessary is that more and more people, with a variety of life-experiences, not only are allowed to study the Scriptures and theology but also to become involved in proclamation. Relinquishment of his prerogatives as a homilist so that others can preach may be for the ordained preacher the best way of proclaiming God in our midst today.

The involvement of the laity in preaching does not just rest on an extraordinary gift of the Spirit or in an extraordinary situation, but is rooted in the God-experience of all the baptized. If ordination traditionally gives the power to preach, today the ordained homilist may be called to relinquish that power for the sake of the fullness of Christian proclamation. While traditionally the power of the ordained was understood as religious power over the laity, today such power must be reconceptualized not as power over others but as enabling power. Such an understanding of power is rooted in the words of Jesus and explored today especially by feminist theology. While the ordained is

responsible that the Word of God is proclaimed, such responsibility does not require that he himself always preaches but that he enables others to do so.

(4). The style of proclamation: Such a communal understanding of proclamation as the right of all the people of God calls into question the "authoritarian one way form" of communication that characterizes preaching today. After lectures we have responses, after press-conferences we have questions, but no one and nothing can challenge and question the proclamation of the homilist. Dialogue homilies that engage the congregation in conversation or communal homilies that engage the congregation in a meditative sharing of experiences and insights are not necessarily "an adding up of zero to zero that equals zero," as someone once suggested, but they are serious attempts to develop a different, more ecclesial rather than clerical style of preaching. We must much more seriously rethink our form and means of proclamation and search for new modes of communication, if the homily should become open to critical dialogue and public discernment of how God can be experienced today in our midst.

II. Interpretation of the Past Experience of the People of God

My emphasis upon the need to be self-critical and to bring to the fore the diversified experiences of others in elucidating the present meaning of the Word of God and the experience of God today can not only be extended to the past, but this model of preaching is derived from the interpretation of the past experiences of God's people in biblical scholarship. Scripture reflects upon and articulates the diverse experiences of God's presence in Israel and among the earliest Christian communities. In order to explore this model of proclamation in Scripture we have (1) to understand the Bible as the formative root-model of Christian faith and community, (2) to ask for the hermeneutical clue

to the correct interpretation of Scripture, and (3) positively use the diversity of contemporary scriptural interpretations.

(1) Biblical studies analyzing the diverse literary forms as well as social world studies reconstructing their diverse historical contexts and cultural milieus have shown the pluriformity and the richness of such experiences of the people of God in the past: not just one literary form but diverse literary forms, different social groups, and even conflicting theological opinions come to expression in our biblical texts. The scriptural texts cannot simply be appealed to as if they provided infallible proof-texts, or as if they provided a monolithic viewpoint that would answer our questions or give us doctrinal solutions for our problems. Instead, the biblical texts present diverse theological insights and diverse practical solutions to theological or communal problems. Since preaching in the present does not rejoice in the diversity of the way we experience God and seek to live as Christians today, homilists are often not able to do justice to the diversity of such faith experiences in the past, expressed in the formative root-model of Scripture. Rather than to adapt Scripture to a monolithic understanding of faith and church, biblical scholarship teaches us to find God in the richness of the diversity and pluriformity of the past.

(2) Yet this pluriformity of the biblical root-model of Christian faith and community raises also a hermeneutical problem. Insofar as Biblical texts reflect diverse experiences in ancient cultures, they are not just liberating texts, but they also codify the oppressive structures and mindsets of these cultures. As one author has put it, the Bible contains not just the "good news" but also some bad news. Or, in other words, the New Testament contains some texts that bring to the fore the Gospel and are given for "the sake of our salvation," whereas other texts express the religious-cultural structures of their times or seek to adapt the early Christian ethos to the societal norms of their times. For instance, in the face of all the destructive powers of modern warfare, the question must be raised whether we still can

pray the curses of the Old Testament psalms against the enemies of Israel. Feminist theology queries whether we can repeat today the patriarchal biblical language for God, while political theology doubts that the biblical language which speaks of God as an absolute monarch is still adequate. If one speaks of scriptural, truth one is speaking of biblical meaning throughout Christian history, of the past as well as of the present, and not just of an isolated stage in this history. Conversely, one can show that certain biblical texts, e.g. the Levitical purity laws or the "household-code" texts of the New Testament, have always functioned to legitimate the patriarchal institution of slavery or the second-class citizenship of women.

The question arises then: how are we to interpret and proclaim these potentially oppressive biblical texts? The homilist cannot simply go on to indiscriminately proclaim all biblical texts as if there were no contradictions among them, or as if there was no distinction between those expressing God's liberating Word of salvation and those expressing oppressive and destructive aspects of the biblical world. The homilist must, therefore, explore the alienating and oppressive aspects and elements in the Bible in order not to preach them as the revelation of God, but to show their human oppresssive character. I personally have attempted elsewhere to elaborate how Vatican II in its document on divine revelation has provided us with a hermeneutical clue to the correct interpretation of the Scriptures. In *Dei Verbum* the Council teaches that Holy Scripture teaches without error that truth which God wanted to put in them for the sake of our salvation. It follows Augustine and Thomas in formulating a criterion that limits revealed truth and inerrancy to matters pertaining to the salvation of the Christian and human community. Salvation must, however, not be reduced to a Platonic sense. It should not be understood just as salvation of the soul but must be conceived in biblical terms as total human salvation and full human rights and wholeness. It cannot be limited to the redemption from personal sin, but, as such

redemption, it must be understood also as redemption and liberation from structural-social sin, such as sexism, racism or classism.

(3) However, the preacher encounters not only the problem of the pluriformity of biblical texts and the problem of the criterion with which to theologically evaluate this diversity, but he encounters also the problem of diverse, often contradictory, exegetical interpretations of these texts. As is well known but often insufficiently reflected upon, a broad theological-social diversity exists among Biblical scholars. This diversity among biblical scholars is due to the different presuppositions, methods, and questions that they bring to the Biblical text. The danger exists that the homilist will select that exegete who is the most "established" or that commentary that fits best into his own theological world-view and personal experience. But it is only through becoming aware of the diverse presuppositions and methods of biblical scholarship, and it is only by taking seriously those interpretations that conflict with one's own theological and social presuppositions and conditions that the homilist is capable of broadening out the experiential and interpretative basis of proclamation. What applies to the present, the need to take into account the experiences of others, also applies to the interpretations of the past. The homilist, therefore, must challenge exegetes and biblical scholars to reflect upon their own experiences and presuppositions and to articulate how they come to play in their interpretations. The diversity of biblical exegesis must be taken into account and articulated if the homily is not to reflect simply a particular experience that finds its expression in a particular but limited interpretation, yet claims objectivity and universal validity for such a particular interpretation.

III. The Move from Experience to Proclamation

In a last step, I want to illustrate how my emphasis on experience as the primary ingredient in the move from study to proclamation would complement, concretize and

broaden Father Burghardt's emphasis on experience and his homiletic suggestions. In his example of how he moves from study to proclamation, he not only carefully describes five steps in the preparation of a homily, but also focuses in the selection of the topic on Mary as the dominating figure of Advent. He informs us that the social location of the homily is the Shrine in Washington and that his choice of the topic was made with a view to the feast of the Immaculate Conception and in the light of a statement of Raymond Brown that three persons, Isaiah, Mary, and John the Baptist dominate the Advent liturgy. Mary reveals, according to him, more remarkably than anyone else how Christians should wait for Christ.

After having selected the topic and studied the Scriptures, Professor Burghardt moves to stage four, that reflects on the details and organization of the homily and the religious response that the homily should call forth. After the study of Scripture and theology, one expects that he connects the topic of the homily with his own or other people's religious experiences. Indeed, in this context he states that he pauses to read Shakespeare, Gerard Manley Hopkins, T.S. Eliot, Tennessee Williams, and to listen to Beethoven, Barber, Tschaikovsky and even to a dash of country music. He listens to the poets and musicians of his culture in order to formulate the details of the homily and to enflesh the topic. Yet I was surprised that he does not think of taking into account the experiences of pregnant women and their sense of self. I wonder whether the male poets and artists he mentions can give his sermon the detail, sensitivity, and insight that he would need for presenting the pregnant Mary of Nazareth as a paradigm of Christian Advent hope. Instead, listening to the experiences of women with pregnancy, their fears, hopes, troubles, and anxieties, their various experiences in giving birth and their exhilaration in touching the newborn child might have illumined and concretized our understanding of Advent waiting. Yet listening to individual experiences does not suffice. One would also need to study feminist analyses, e.g., Adrienne Rich's book on the institution of motherhood in patriarchal society, to

learn how the experience of motherhood is structurally and societally mediated and conditioned. One might also listen to single mothers on welfare or to the woman at the checkout counter trying to feed and clothe their children. If the word has to become flesh in the homily, then it must become flesh in the particular experiences of those about whom the homily speaks. And the Mary of Advent is the pregnant Mary, the unwed mother.

This is not to criticize Father Burghardt's way of procedure — indeed if only more sermons reflected such high literary standards and artistic sources. My point is mainly to emphasize the importance of reflecting upon and listening to different experiences, especially those pertinent to the theme of the sermon. Moving from such attentive listening to women's personal and structural experiences with motherhood, the Lukan texts on Mary come to new life. Mary, and not Joseph, is the morally responsible agent in becoming pregnant. The gospel stresses her freedom of choice. She does not remain isolated but seeks support from another woman, Elizabeth. She has to learn that not natural family bonds and the claims of motherhood but the issues of God determine her relationship to her child. Her calling is not just motherhood but creative discipleship. As such a spirit-filled person, the pregnant Mary announces the future of God to the heavy laden and downtrodden in the *Magnificat*. The future of God's salvation and wholeness is not to be awaited passively and without our active involvement, but it is being born among us today from our flesh and blood, from our commitments and our struggles today. It is fashioned and becomes form as the hope for those who are without hope. In short, it is by articulating the pertinent experiences of women as the people of God that this homily on the Mary of Advent can elicit the faith response that the homily intends.

These brief remarks do not mean in any way to detract from the persuasiveness of Father Burghardt's suggestions, but they merely seek to underline how the interpretation of present and past experience demands that the homilist becomes acutely aware that not he himself, and not he

alone, but in many cases, others may have the key to what the meaning of the word of God is for us today. It was in this light that I have suggested that an interpretation of Mary's experience during Advent can only take place with references to the personally and structurally reflected experiences of women among God's people. In short, the "silenced majority" must be heard and allowed into "speech" again if the richness and fullness of God's presence with us should be articulated and proclaimed today. The right of the baptized to proclamation is not just charismatic and extraordinary, but it must become the essential ingredient of all preaching, if the experience of God in our midst should be proclaimed in its fullness. While the ordained have the call and duty to ensure that proclamation takes place, all the people of God — ordained or not — are called to proclaim the great and marvelous deeds of God in Christ for our world and church.

Preaching In The Acts Of The Apostles
Raymond E. Brown, S.S.

Response
James M. Reese, O.S.F.S.

Preaching In The Acts Of The Apostles
Raymond E. Brown, S.S.

Prefatory Remarks

Before I begin to speak on "Preaching in the Acts of the Apostles," I wish to call attention to the fact that this is a *Word of God Institute*. That demands a very careful consideration of what we mean by the word of God. I have written on this subject at length elsewhere,[1] and so here I wish only to issue a reminder that speaking words is a *human* action. When one refers to God as speaking, one is no less anthropomorphic than when one refers to God as smelling or walking. Therefore, word of God means the *human word* of Almighty God; and every such word, written or spoken, is time-conditioned. Accordingly, we cannot escape the impact of biblical criticism on the sermons in the Acts of the Apostles. Any attempt to bypass biblical criticism is an attempt to remove the Scriptures from the human sphere and thus to distort the relationship between human word and divine revelation. We must maintain a delicate balance between acknowledging the deeply conditioned and limited

---

[1] See my article on "Biblical Reflections on Scripture as the Word of God," *Theological Studies* 42 (1981) 3-19, reprinted as the first chapter in my book *The Critical Meaning of the Bible* (New York: Paulist, 1981) 1-22.

outlook of the biblical writers and the unique divine origins of what they wrote. The Scriptures present to us a paradox similar to that of a preexistent Son of God who had to learn obedience and was like us in everything except sin.

Going beyond this, but still in fidelity to biblical criticism, when I begin to speak of preaching in the Acts of the Apostles, I am very conscious that in the sermons we do not necessarily have the words of Peter or Paul or Stephen.[2] We have unquestionably the words of the unknown author of the Book of Acts who dramatizes for his readers Peter and Paul and Stephen speaking on certain occasions. (We can only guess about his sources and their accuracy; but the primary interest of an interpreter is not sources but what the author of the Book of Acts has written.) I insist on this because otherwise one might get the facile impression that we are actually reading the first sermons ever given by Christians. We are not. We are reading sermons composed by an author, perhaps in the 80s of the first century, to convey a message to his audience. Note: "to *his* audience." We are not hearing sermons addressed to us, but sermons once addressed to an audience in the 80s. The idea that the Scriptures are written *to* us is a mistake that leads to the distortion of the word of God. The Scriptures have meaning *for* us, but they were written to audiences that lived at the time of their authors. These remarks may seem very somber at the beginning of a *Word of God Institute*, but I feel that today "the word of God" encounters great dangers. On the one hand, the recognition through biblical criticism that the Scriptures are time-conditioned words leads some to deny the "of God" in the word of God. On the other hand, among those who are interested in the word of God, a greater danger is the temptation to avoid or deny biblical criticism and thus to distort the "word" element in the word of God.

Having stressed the historical conditioning of the preaching in the Book of Acts, allow me to draw another observa-

---

[2]In this address I shall concentrate on the sermons of Peter in Acts, chaps. 2,3,5, 10; of Paul in chaps. 13-17; and of Stephen in chap. 7.

tion from the fact that this is a *Word of God Institute*. The Hebrew *dabar* that we translate as "word," has a much wider meaning, including "thing" and "action." If one would study the Book of Acts, one must realize that preaching is only a partial element of what an author with a biblical background would think of by the "word" of God. Acts describes the *actions* of the apostolic preachers, including their healings of the sick, their raisings of the dead, their sufferings, and even their martyrdoms. Such an emphasis on actions is important to remember in an institute on preaching. Frankly, I rejoice in the fact that Roman Catholic clergy are not called preachers. The failure to designate them thus may indicate all too sadly that Catholics do not put enough emphasis on preaching, but there is a greater distortion involved in identifying clergy as if their only task were to preach. The early Christian proclaimers of the Good News did more than preach, and we had better do more in this world than preach if we wish to be proclaimers of the word of God. As has often been said, the God of Israel is a God who acts and not simply a God who speaks. Both descriptions are anthropomorphic, but nevertheless together they convey the truth that those who proclaim the God of Israel and the Father of Jesus Christ had better be as concerned about action as about preaching.

General Remarks on the Sermons

After such preliminary cautions I now move toward my main concern: the sermons in the Acts of the Apostles. Since they are all compositions of the author of Acts, not surprisingly there are common features. The surprise is rather the amount of diversity we find among the sermons. Perhaps such diversity is explicable because the author had sources reflecting diverse traditions, but just as plausible is the thesis that the author had great skill in adjusting his sermon

composition to different situations. In either case, the diversity of the sermons in Acts teaches us something about preaching the word of God. There is no exclusive way to preach the word of God. Rather, with all its splendor, the word of God requires a diversity of presentation, reflecting different ways in which God's revelation can have meaning in human life.

First, there is diversity on the part of the preacher. The author of Acts describes Peter on several occasions going to the Temple in Jerusalem and preaching Jesus Christ there (3:1; 5:12). The author makes it clear that the setting is part of the piety of the apostles who were among those whom he describes as "every day in the Temple" (5:42). Nevertheless, the author also gives us a sermon by Stephen who does not believe that God dwells in the Temple. Rather, in building the Temple the Israelites were offending against the will of God who does not dwell in human houses; and thus they were resisting the Holy Spirit (7:48-51). In other words Acts describes as proclaiming the word of God with equal piety preachers whose views on the relation of the Christian message to the Jerusalem Temple were virtually contradictory. (The attitude of the author of Acts may not be far from that of Paul in Phil 2:15-18: "Some indeed preach Christ from envy and rivalry, but others from good will.... What then? Only that in every way...Christ is proclaimed.") Whether or not the preachers of Acts had the same view of the Jerusalem Temple, they shared a view of the centrality of Christ; and for Acts that centrality was all important in evaluating their proclamation of the word. I point to this diversity and centrality as of possible value for our preaching today. Not every view can be proclaimed from our pulpits; but particularly in Roman Catholicism the desire for absolute uniformity in the conception of the Christian message may not be true to the New Testament itself which allowed a diversity among Christians who still shared *koinōnia*, or "communion," with one another. We must realize that on many theological issues Peter and Paul and Stephen could disagree violently, and yet they were all esteemed by the author of Acts as great Christian witnesses and

preachers. A range of diversity is both allowed and demanded by the word of God.

A second aspect of the diversity in Acts, this time affecting the audience, is reflected in Paul's preaching in chap. 13 to the "men of Israel," where he introduces his words about Christ by reciting the history of Israel.[3] In Acts 17 the same Paul addresses the "men of Athens," speaking to them about the Lord of heaven and earth who gives life to all and governs the course of all nations. In other words, for the author of Acts there are two different Pauline prefaces to the Christian proclamation, one for Jews, the other for Gentiles. I have insisted from the beginning that the word of God depends not only on God but also on the human beings for whom this has to be a word. Woe to preachers if it is not "of God," but also woe to them if it is not truly a word because it has not been made meaningful to the audience to whom they address their divine message.

Granted that the "men of Athens" can be addressed without a recitation of what we may call the Old Testament story, it is still remarkable how often the author of Acts makes the Old Testament story a part of the preaching almost equal in length to the story of Jesus Christ. In Acts 2 Peter does not specifically turn his message to Jesus of Nazareth until he has recalled the words of Joel the prophet; and even when he does turn to Jesus, the words of the psalmist are part of the message about Jesus. In Acts 7 Stephen traces the story of Israel from Abraham to Solomon in a long sermon that never even gets to Jesus Christ other than by implication. In Acts 13 Paul spends more than half his sermon on what the God of Israel has done before he announces that this God has brought to Israel "a Savior, Jesus." These are sermons that Acts addresses to the Jews or to "men of Israel," but perhaps one can draw from them implications for sermons addressed to the people of God today, a people for whom the Old Testament is by church teaching as much the Scriptures of God as

---

[3] The translation "men" is warranted, not careless, here because the Greek is *andres*, not *anthrōpoi*.

the New Testament. Too often for Christians the proclamation of the word means the proclamation of the Jesus story. Yet that story can be easily misconstrued and distorted if one does not also recite the story of Israel. For instance, the triumph of what has been accomplished in Jesus Christ and the success it should have in the world is a dangerous message if one has not heard the story of God's salvific acts in Israel, including the decimation of His people and the loss of the land and of the Temple. The word of God can be as truly proclaimed in defeat as in victory when that defeat warns us of the possibility of confusing our success with what God regards as success. Such a message does not always become clear in the New Testament, written in a short period of spreading and seemingly victorious faith; it comes through very clearly in the Old Testament story, a millennium long, which allows us to see the interplay between God's message and human appropriation and distortion.

The Message about Christ

While insisting on the importance of the Old Testament preface, one would have to say that a comparison of the main sermons in Acts leads firmly to the centrality of Jesus Christ in the proclamation of the word. What God has done in Christ from the time of his baptism through mighty deeds, leading to the crucifixion of Christ by men and his resurrection by God — this is certainly for the author of Acts the heart of the message. The very fact that the author mentions that those who accepted this proclamation were soon called Christians means that it is inconceivable that Christ is not the primary proclamation. If I may be permitted to draw from this a lesson for our proclamation today, I would insist that what God did in Jesus Christ must still be the heart of our message. That does not mean that we can ignore implications about what *we are to do* toward God and toward humanity; but all such obligation of action

depends on understanding and believing in Jesus Christ. It would be fascinating to take a poll of the people in our churches and ask them what it means today to be a Christian. Many "Bible Christians" might answer, "Have faith in Jesus as Savior," and fail to include the obligation of loving others. A greater number, not doctrinally concerned, might answer in existential terms about what one must do, for instance, in terms of loving one's neighbor. Existential demand is urgent — Christians must love — but our *behavior is not a sufficiently differentiating element in the definition of a Christian.* Christians are those who have a clear faith about Jesus of Nazareth, that he is the Christ, the Messiah of God. Any definition of a Christian that does not involve a clear proclamation of who Jesus is (alongside the obligation of loving) fails the criterion of the first proclamations of Christianity. Indeed, in this aspect, Christianity has a certain uniqueness among the religions of the world. For all their reverence for Moses, Jews would not define their religion in terms of who Moses is. Muslims resent the appellation "Mohammedans" because they regard this as a distortion of their religion along the lines of Christian thought patterns: their primary faith is about Allah for whom Mohammed was a prophet. But we Christians are people whose definition comes, not simply in terms of what we say about God, but in terms of what we say about Jesus, precisely because we think that we cannot understand God unless we understand who Jesus was and is. The failure to proclaim Jesus and what God did in him will eviscerate the Christian proclamation of the word of God.

In the sermons of Acts, it is clear that the crucifixion and resurrection represent the heart of the story of Jesus. Particularly from Acts 2 and Acts 10 we can learn a lesson about what it means to make Jesus Christ the center of the proclamation. One cannot proclaim him without the resurrection, which was God's vindication of Jesus. The oldest formulations of the Christian creedal faith may be imbedded in these sermons in the Book of Acts, particularly in the antithesis: You killed him, but God raised him up. These proclaim a divine action and a divine victory. Such a proclamation

shows that Christianity is not primarily a religion of human possibilities or of what we can do; it is primarily a proclamation of God's action and of His grace reversing our sinfulness and weakness.

If the resurrection is the divine action most clearly expressing this victory, that resurrection in the sermons of Acts makes little sense without the cross. At times, when I wish to portray this point bluntly, I tell people that Jesus could have been victorious over death if he died of a heart attack on the shores of the Lake of Galilee and if subsequently God raised him up; but then Christianity would be a different religion. The author of Acts caught the essential contrast, the essential paradox of Christianity, namely, victory *after the disgraceful kind of death Jesus died.* Dying after being betrayed by his disciple and rejected by the religious leaders was part of Jesus' revelation of God's kingdom. It is no accident that, when we have sought visually to portray Christianity, the cross has been our clearest sign. Without the resurrection the cross would be meaningless; but without the cross the resurrection might confirm a triumphalistic human understanding of God, rather than God's self-understanding.

Even if the cross and the resurrection are the central aspect of the christology of the sermons in Acts, the ministry of Jesus is also important. In the New Testament, Paul is the author who most uses the word "gospel"; yet Paul rarely quotes the words or deeds of the ministry of Jesus. His concentration is on the death and resurrection of Jesus: "Put to death for our trespasses and raised for our justification" (Rom 4:25). Nevertheless, it seems that the church has not accepted the narrow confines of the Pauline understanding of gospel; for she has placed in the canon of the New Testament before the Pauline letters four other works entitled "Gospels." They concentrate on the ministry of Jesus and indeed give greater proportion to that ministry than to the story of the cross and resurrection. For most people, a reference to a Gospel is a reference to one of these four works. Perhaps this attitude is adumbrated in Acts in the sermons that tell first of what God did in Jesus from the

time of the baptism before they turn to the crucifixion and resurrection. For instance, the sermon in Acts 2 speaks of "mighty wonders and works and signs which God did through him in your midst." The sermon in Acts 10 speaks of his "being anointed with the Holy Spirit and with power" and his "doing good and healing all that were afflicted." Indeed, if as I have said already, one cannot understand the resurrection properly without the cross, one cannot understand either the cross or the resurrection without understanding the Jesus who reached out to heal the sick and to give mobility to the lame. Moreover, if one wishes to go beyond the sermons of Acts, I would argue that one cannot understand the cross and resurrection properly without realizing that it is the death and victory of one who proclaimed God's blessing to the poor and the oppressed. In all this, we are taught the centrality of the *whole picture* of Jesus Christ, his life, death, and resurrection.

Reaction to the Message

If this is the fundamental Christian proclamation, if this is the gospel, if this is the word of God understood both as deed and preached word (the Hebrew *dabar* that I mentioned above), the sermon in Acts 2 does not leave us without a description of the necessary reaction to the proclamation or gospel or word of God. In 2:37 those who hear the message of Peter say to him and to the rest of the apostles, "Brothers, what shall we do?" The first demand that Peter places by way of response is *Metanoēsate*. Most translations render this as "Repent"; a few go further and translate it as "Change your lives." The literal Greek meaning of *metanoein*, however, is "to change one's mind." Unless we understand the fullness of that term we cannot understand why or how the word of God constitutes an offense. It is true that if one is a serious sinner, "to change one's mind" or "to change one's way of thinking" means "to repent" or "to change one's way of living." But most proclamation of the word of God in preaching today is addressed to those who are not

conscious of being serious sinners. Is either the preacher or the audience to think that the obligations of *metanoein* have been accomplished simply because serious sin is not an issue? Such misapprehension will not occur if we understand the word to mean "to change one's mind."

Religious people think they know what God wants. If one suggests to such people that it is necessary to change one's mind about what God wants in order to hear the word of God, then the offense of the Gospel becomes clear. We remember that Jesus had few problems with sinners; they seem to have been relatively open to his message. His greatest problem was with religious people who knew already what God wanted and were therefore offended by hearing a different message from Jesus. The Christian preachers in the Book of Acts are portrayed as placing the same demand that Jesus placed. True, they placed this demand upon people who were hearing the gospel for the first time; but one may well ask if *Metanoēsate* is not an enduring demand for hearing the gospel at any time. The preacher who asks people to change their minds is often the preacher who will be castigated for disturbing the people, precisely because it is not sufficiently stressed, when we teach religion, that Jesus was a disturbing figure and that his message presented faithfully will inevitably disturb. That disturbance does not touch simply sinful behavior but also wrong conceptions of God's set of values.

I see this as a particular problem in the preaching experience of Roman Catholics. We have been emphatic that we have a set of answers and that those need to be repeated and passed on from generation to generation. The whole catechism approach implies that. I do not deny that we have a continuous truth, but that truth needs to be rephrased in every generation if it is to be effective. The idea of rephrasing revealed truth is *not* the innovation of radical theologians. The Roman Holy Office or Doctrinal Congregation itself has recognized that divine truths are often phrased in the changeable conceptions of a given epoch and may need to be rephrased in order to convey their message to people at

another time.[4] Walking the narrow line between carelessly or needlessly disturbing people and the necessary challenge and disturbance caused by the gospel properly preached is a very difficult task — a task not helped by ultraconservatives who charge every new presentation or new idea with being dangerous. The gospel insistence on changing one's mind repeated after the sermon in Acts 2 is an enduring statement that the greatest danger facing religion is *not* the danger of new ideas; it is *the danger of no ideas at all.* Too often those who have the official task of proclaiming the word of God see no danger if people are passively content in their religion. They see a greater danger when people are restive about what they hear and when they ask themselves and others challenging questions. Such a fearful attitude is not faithful to the fundamental reaction demanded by the preaching of Jesus and his followers in terms of *metanoein.*

After insisting on repentance or change of mind, according to Acts 2:38, Peter places a demand that Jesus is never portrayed as placing during his public ministry, namely, the demand to be baptized.[5] Strangely, in all four gospels only once is Jesus ever portrayed as baptizing people (John 3:22) and the fact that he did baptize is immediately thereafter denied in John 4:2. Jesus was not a baptizer; yet those who proclaimed his gospel insisted on the necessity of being baptized. One sees here a new aspect of the proclamation of the gospel. Even though there was a collective force to the gospel preached by Jesus in his lifetime, he simply presupposed Israel and the whole people of God as the context of his message. Hence, although he associated with himself a

---

[4] I have reprinted the pertinent section of *Mysterium Ecclesiae* (1973) as an appendix to *Biblical Reflections on Crises Facing the Church* (New York: Paulist, 1975) 116-118.

[5] The command to go and baptize all nations, peculiar to Matthew (28:19) is post-resurrectional. It raises enormous historical problems if taken as a historical saying of Jesus known to his followers from the beginning of the church. See the article cited in note 1 above (*Critical Meaning* 13-14).

group of disciples, Jesus was not clearly forming *an organized society* by his preaching; there was no "church" in his public ministry; there was Israel which he was calling to change its mind. Yet Acts portrays the Christian preachers as immediately beginning to form a society within Israel. The insistence on baptism is a very important mark of the structuring of a society — one now has a way of knowing openly those who accepted the proclamation. The believers are baptized visibly and thus enter a *koinōnia*, "communion" with one another. This may be one aspect of the word of God that is sometimes neglected in the modern conception of the desirable effects of preaching. The proclamation of Christianity has as its goal not simply personal conversion or personal change of mind; it has as its goal the formation and development of the church, the people of God. It is true that in the Gospel of John baptism is portrayed in terms of being begotten from above or born again of water and spirit; but that is not the portrayal in Acts. For the author of Acts baptism involves acceptance into a community, and Christianity is a communitarian religion. To all those people who say, "Jesus is my personal savior," I would insist (without negating the personal element in the salvation wrought by Jesus) that our primary understanding must be that of Jesus *saving a people*. This emphasis makes proclaiming the word of God or preaching the Gospel a church-related task, so that the effectiveness of preaching must be evaluated in terms not simply of how many hearts are touched, but also of how the church is built up.

The demand to be baptized in Acts 2:38 is continued with a further comment about purpose: "Be baptized every one of you in the name of Jesus Christ for the forgiveness of your sins." I spoke as strongly as I could above of the centrality of belief in Jesus Christ as part of the definition of a Christian. If baptism has its communal effect, that effect is related to the fact that the person to be baptized makes a confession of who Jesus is, of his name: He is the Christ (Messiah), the Lord, the Savior, the Son of God (Acts 2:36; 5:31; 13:33). And this baptism and confession of Jesus Christ is accom-

panied by the forgiveness of sins. The collective aspect of baptism does not obscure its personal effect; and that effect is forgiveness of sins and thus the possibility of holiness. A proclamation of the word of God that involves change of mind and baptism would still not be complete unless it also effected at least incipiently the ultimate demand of the God of Israel: "You must be holy because I the Lord your God am holy" (Lev 19:2; I Peter I:16). The holiness of the individual and the holiness of the people with whom that individual is joined in *koinōnia* through baptism are the fruit of the life, death, and resurrection of Jesus which is the substance of the Christian preaching. Very often one conceives the proclamation of the word as changing the world. That role may be true; but unless we see the change in terms of holiness, we have not understood how the world must ultimately reflect the image and likeness of God.

The last part of the demand and the promise that follow the first sermon in the Book of Acts is this: "You shall receive the gift of the Holy Spirit." The Spirit is the final step in the work of Jesus. The ultimate actions that crown his ministry include not only crucifixion and resurrection, but also the giving of the Spirit. If the proclamation of the word is the continuity of his work, it must be related to the gift of the Spirit. A preacher like Stephen is described as "full of the Spirit" (Acts 7:54); but it is never suggested that the preacher gives the Spirit. The gift of the Spirit is from God; the preacher opens the hearts of his hearers to receive the divine gift. That may be an important observation at a time when we are very concerned about the effectiveness of preaching. No doubt the skills of the preacher are important; yet we must be wary of Madison Avenue's standards of promoting effectiveness, embodied for many in the nattily-dressed TV preacher, with carefully styled hair, clutching his King James Bible amid banks of flowers and a background of blond gospel singers. The ultimate effectiveness of preaching is in the hands of God whose gift of the Spirit often surprises in the direction it takes — "The Spirit/wind blows where it wills" (John 3:8).

In concluding, I am sure that, based on a study of Acts, many other observations might be made about preaching, but the ones I have made are in my judgment important both in Acts and for modern preaching. Let me list them:

-- a firm grasp of the time-conditioned character of the biblical accounts;
-- an understanding that the word (*dabar*) of God is larger than preaching or the spoken word;
-- the tolerability and even necessity of somewhat diverse positions held by the preachers so that the fullness of the divine subject may be mirrored;
-- the need to adapt the message to different audiences so that it may be a meaningful word;
-- the priority, necessity, and corrective value of the story of Israel without which Christ is easily misunderstood;
-- the centrality of what God has done *in Christ* if a message is to be distinctively Christian;
-- the different respective roles of resurrection, crucifixion, and ministry of Jesus in preaching the whole Christ — it was a crucified one who was raised, and he was crucified because he had offered the kingdom to those who by human standards were to be rejected;
-- the fundamental reaction to an evaluation of what the Christ means is *metanoia*, "change of mind," a task no less difficult for religious people today than it was in the time of Jesus;
-- that reaction must lead the hearers into a relation with the church and its sacraments;
-- the goal of the preaching is to bring about holiness through the forgiveness of sins and God's somewhat unpredictable gift of the Spirit.

In reflecting on the list, one cannot help being astonished by the profundity of the message and the reactions demanded in the early sermons described in Acts. If the author was partially historical and the sermons reflect not only the 80s but something of the 30s and 40s, the first preachers accomplished a great task. They did not preach the kingdom simply as Jesus preached it; they kept the

message alive by ingeniously translating it into another idiom. They preached the kingdom by preaching Christ as they saw him. That may leave us with a final observation about subsequent preaching — final but paradoxically first in the order of procedure. One cannot preach unless one rethinks what one has grasped. All the slogans, "Preach only what is in the Bible," or, "Preach only what the Church teaches," are simplistic if they do not recognize the need for translating what has been received into a new idiom to keep it alive. If there is much bad preaching in Roman Catholicism, the most basic difficulty is not the ignorance of the preacher, nor the lack of oratorical skills; it is the failure to have thought through the biblical or church tradition to the point where it means something vital to the preachers themselves and to the audience. We can be deeply thankful that, according to the evidence of Acts, the first preachers were not simply people who transmitted what Jesus taught; they were people who thought about what he meant.

Response
James M. Reese, O.S.F.S.

These masterful reflections on preaching in Acts of the Apostles offer many opportunities for reflection. Remembering the setting of this talk — as Fr. Brown does in his prefatory remarks — I shall direct my response to two aspects: 1) to elaborate some implications for preachers that flow from his descriptions of the sermons in Acts; 2) to make specific observations on three phrases that might come as a surprise to his listeners.

1. Implications for Preachers

As a result of the First National Congress on the Word of God in Washington, D. C., "The Burning Word" feature was started in *The Bible Today*. As a result of an agreement between Fr. John Burke, O.P., and the late Fr. Eugene Maly, first editor of *The Bible Today*, I had the privilege of editing that feature for eight years. After reading Fr. Brown's talk, I went back to my own introductory article in the November 1973 issue, entitled "Preaching the Burning Word." I was struck by how well it speaks to the task of adapting biblical scholarship to the ministry of preaching. Fr. Brown focuses attention on one aspect of that task when

he calls attention to the difference between the way Peter
and Paul spoke and the way their sermons are presented in
Acts. He directs attention to "what the author of the Book
of Acts has written...to *his* audience."

In other words, the biblical presentation is "time-
conditioned." In asking preachers to take seriously the gap
between the way an author in the first century of the Christian era writes and the world of contemporary society, Fr.
Brown makes a point similar to advice given by Pope Paul
VI to Italian biblical scholars gathered in Rome on September 25, 1970. In my presentation of "The Burning Word"
program I referred to that talk, which was published in
Osservatore Romano on October 8, 1970. The Holy Father
stressed the need of hermeneutics, that is, "the study of the
means and the interpretative process itself in the widest
sense." He reminded his audience that they have to look not
merely at the words of the text but at the "roots, conditions
and times" they make the text speak to. To fulfill this task
they "need to seek a certain connaturality of interest and
problems with the argument of the text."

Why is this? The preexistent Word of God became incarnate in a particular historical period with its own language,
customs, traditions and culture. And yet he came not for
one people or one generation only but for the salvation of all
humanity. So preachers must make the gospel message
"present whole and entire not just to man in general but to
man of today, to whom the message is announced now." Fr.
Brown points out that the sermons in Acts provide a basis
for helping preachers fulfill this responsibility by their very
"diversity." He takes pains to show this diversity has several
implications: it points not only to "diverse traditions" but
also to "great skill in adjusting his sermon composition to
different situations." Furthermore, the two "different Pauline prefaces to the Christian proclamation, one for Jews,
the other for gentiles," show that the author adapted his
approach to the situation of hearers.

Comparable adaptation of the saving word becomes even
more necessary as the gap between the world of the original
apostles and the society in which believers live widens. Fr.

Brown's reminder that today's preachers must study and reflect is in line with Pope Paul VI's observation, "Fidelity to modern man is demanding and difficult, but it is necessary."

Brown's careful analysis of the Book of Acts finds that the key to open its riches is "the centrality of Jesus Christ." He does not equate that centrality with "the Jesus story." On the contrary, Jesus Christ is correctly understood and believed only as the central figure in relation to the "story of God's salvific acts in Israel." The Jewish Scriptures remain an essential part of the story of the people of God today. Acts draws upon them to present Christian preaching as a "message about Christ," whose earthly life and teaching, death and resurrection give Christian faith a "uniqueness among religions of the world." As Brown states it, Christianity "is primarily a proclamation of God's action and of His grace reversing our sinfulness and weakness."

He urges preachers to build upon what God has done in Christ for the salvation of the world. To do so is to remember that to be a Christian is to be the bearer of a unique faith. Preachers nourish that faith by constantly directing believers to open their minds and hearts to what Jesus did to fulfill his mission as "the Christ, the Messiah of God." The actual content of most preaching flows from the canonical accounts of the ministry of Jesus in the four gospels. These provide the principal scriptural reading at each eucharistic celebration.

By embodying the early Church's faith in Jesus Christ, the gospels communicate what Brown happily calls "God's self-understanding." That expression promises profound insight into the fruitfulness of living faith. Faith is ultimately God's self-giving, the availability of God's saving power. But faith is also a human response nourished by living contact with the abiding presence of Jesus in word and sacrament. Traditionally Christians have expressed this mutuality of faith by exalting the Cross. This mysterious sign stretches vertically to link heaven and earth and horizontally to embrace all humanity.

As sign of "one who proclaimed God's blessing to the

poor and the oppressed," the Cross demands response. Brown shows its importance in the life of believers by devoting the final third of his address to spelling out what God asks of them. In this context he explains both the continuous need of preaching and the daily attitude of mind and heart transformed by the divine Word. Just as the "Christian preachers in the Book of Acts" made "the same demand that Jesus placed," so Christian preachers today must proclaim that God still "asks people to change their mind." They are able to do so not of their own power in a superficial way but only through the creative power of God's Word.

In this section Fr. Brown touches on the responsibility of preachers to their contemporary hearers, a duty that Pope Paul VI discussed in his talk quoted above. He pointed out the prevailing mentality that "demands clear and simple notions about everything and judges everything in terms of the horizon of human powers of understanding." To meet these severe demands preachers must cultivate imagination and resourcefulness. No wonder the Pope concludes that "to interpret and explain the Scripture's permanent message is of urgent and exciting topicality." For a fruitful ministry preachers must experience how modern persons think and feel and react.

In particular, the overwhelming problems of peace and justice that face humanity have created what I pointed to as "a pessimism about mankind's future." This oppressive atmosphere has created a "greater sense of urgency" among many preachers, who often support each other in preparing homilies. But the danger I referred to remains: that they will experience "no response, no change of attitude" and so will become discouraged.

Fr. Brown calls this situation a "fearful attitude" toward the Word. He points out that it can exist not only in the faithful but even in those "who have the official task of proclaiming the word of God." He warns that overstress on personal salvation could obscure the truth that "Christianity is a communitarian religion." I recommend that all of us reflect on his insights about the "collective aspect of baptism" and the holiness it communicates and generates.

In this context it is clear that the activity of *metanoein* or changing one's mind involves the experience of religious conversion and the quest for growth in union with God's will for our salvation. "The Burning Word" program, sponsored by the Word of God Institute, built upon the providential role of preachers to build up the common faith of the Church. Every preacher is necessarily a performer in the linguistic sense of handling "performative" speech — to use the term of J. L. Austin. For an appreciation of the power of language to accomplish something, preachers would do well to study Austin's exciting book entitled *How to Do Things with Words* (Oxford: University Press, 1965).

Another essential step in a fruitful response to this masterful description of Preaching in Acts of the Apostles will be for preachers to prioritize for themselves the nine summary observations of Fr. Brown. Each preacher will do well to wrestle with that list in personal reflection. It is an excellent checklist to evaluate present attitudes and to discern strengths and weaknesses one has as a communicator of the Word. Facility in handling Scripture frees preachers to devote their energy to serving the people of God.

2. Observations on Specific Expressions

Now I shall comment briefly on three specific elements in the talk that may come as new information to hearers. Again, I shall relate them to the role of preaching.

The first item is the reference to "the unknown author of the Book of Acts." Some readers may have wondered, "Why did he say that? I thought Luke wrote Acts." This is the kind of information that often creates a defensive reaction in hearers. My concern is to point out how this change of outlook relates to the view of the Bible as word of God. Some Catholics feel the use of critical research downgrades the divine element of Scripture. For example, recently I was teaching how the parables of Jesus are used differently by each of the three synoptic evangelists. One student protested

that, no matter how they were used, the parables were still inspired and should be presented as such. This illustrates the tension many feel between traditional presentation and modern biblical criticism.

Preachers need to keep a sense of the unity of the divine and the human element in the production of the Bible. While holding fast to the inspiration of Scripture, we should remember that the technical term "divinely inspired" appears in the Bible only in 2 Timothy 3:16. Theologians still wrestle with that concept. But as members of a free society, we rebel against any presentation of inspiration that pictures God as "using" human beings like tools. A better approach is to recognize that ancient religious authors did not view themselves as modern novelists, as creating original works of art. On the contrary, biblical writers wanted to be the voice of authentic tradition and to hide their identity behind the community.

The early Church attached names to the gospels more to identify them with various streams of apostolic tradition than to call attention to any particular individual. The introductory volume to the New Testament Message commentary by Daniel J. Harrington (Wilmington, DE: Michael Glazier, 1979) gives a clear presentation of the various kinds of criticism involved in dealing with the New Testament. Preachers can learn from his careful presentation not so much for direct use in homilies as to increase their awareness of the resources they need to do justice to communicating God's saving message.

A second statement that may have come as a surprise is Fr. Brown's reminder: the "idea that the Scriptures were written *to* us is a mistake." This comment is a way of dramatizing the need for some knowledge of both history and language on the part of all who read Scripture. Bible translators have been aware of this need for a long time, and I called attention to it in my introduction to "The Burning Word" series. There I wrote, "Translators like Eugene A. Nida are showing how an appreciation of language can enrich understanding of the Bible." He has taken the lead in

producing a series of Translator's Handbooks that include insights into how the text works — a feature often overlooked in other commentaries. One point that Nida stresses is the importance of dealing with words in context. Since words are signs, they have meaning only in a system. This feature of language is important for understanding the thrust of *metanoein* that Fr. Brown talked about.

Biblical writers intended to make saving truth available to those believers who never saw the Lord Jesus or his apostles. But they did not know the problems of a computer society or the idioms of modern languages. So they did not write *to* us directly. If their writings are to be lifegiving *for* us, preachers must become bridges that stretch their message across the centuries. Pope Paul VI pointed out this responsibility to biblical instructors when he said, "Interpretation has not fulfilled its task until it has demonstrated how the meaning of Scripture may be referred to the present salvific moment, that is, until it has brought the application to the present circumstances of the Church and the World."

Third and last, listeners may have been surprised to hear concentration on "the death and resurrection of Jesus" spoken of as forming "the narrow confines of the Pauline understanding of the Gospel." Again, this carefully crafted phrase serves to specify what Fr. Brown has implied throughout his presentation, namely, that the New Testament was the production of the early Church. Paul's letters are only a part of this Christian collection, and its 27 writings in turn are only part of the entire library accepted by the Church as its official Scriptures. A real danger exists that individual believers will shrink the great vision of Scripture to a private canon, a list of one's favorite passages. As he puts it, "Religious people think they know what God wants," and the religious Jews of his time were "offended by hearing a different message from Jesus."

We all probably have our favorite scriptural author, but that must not blind us to the total truth of God's saving plan, what Acts calls "God's design in its entirety" (20:27). The Bible presents this design from a variety of angles. Preachers

continue to make it available by "rephrasing revealed truth" in ways that move hearers to repentance and newness of life. Fr. Brown's description of preaching in the Book of Acts encourages preachers to keep the big picture in focus as they carry out their task in building up the Church of God.

Preaching As Food For Thought And Action In The Church
Edward K. Braxton

Response
Fred B. Craddock

Preaching As Food For Thought
And Action In The Church

Edward K. Braxton

I. Introduction

It happens every Sunday. People make their way from all over town to a singular building that oftentimes sits empty for the rest of the week. The seats are hard and uncomfortable. The lighting and decorations may leave something to be desired and, inevitably, the microphone and speaker system are inadequate. No matter. At a certain moment a man, or even a woman, ascends the stairs and commences a great discourse. Fifteen minutes and many yawns and coughs later, it is over. Call it a sermon, call it a homily, call it what you will. Another experience of Christian preaching has been endured and survived by preacher and people alike.

Happily, this caricature does not apply to every church congregation. There are many places where Catholic preachers have grown immensely in their appreciation of the importance of preaching. And with the help of an aggressive congregation, they have refined their Sunday proclamation to a pastoral art. But there are still far too many Catholic parishes where priests and people alike consider the Sunday sermon to be a weekly chore to be put

behind them as quickly as possible. As a result, the congregation as well as the preacher are impoverished.

What is the relationship between preaching and our growth as the people of God? Does preaching nourish the faith of the contemporary Christian? How ought we to preach if we wish to contribute to the ongoing growth and development of the faith life of individual Christians and whole ecclesial communities?

These are the questions before us this afternoon.

These questions in turn raise others: "What is preaching?" and "What is faith?" No doubt we each have a working understanding of what preaching is and several of the presentations this week are designed to enrich that understanding. However, we cannot proceed to reflect on the role of preaching in the development of faith without some common understanding of just what faith is.

II. Faith: A Personal Call to Conversion

What really do we mean by faith? We often hear such expressions as: "Keep the faith." "Practice the faith." "Don't lose your faith." "They have fallen away from the faith." What precisely are we talking about when we say this?

Is faith, in its most fundamental form, the intellectual acceptance of a body of teachings about: the existence of God, Father, Son and Spirit; the content of Revelation; the truth of Scripture; the purpose of the Catholic Church; the essence of the priesthood; the importance of the Sacraments; the limits of ecumenism; the extent of the role of women in the Church; the reality of sin and grace; the nature of hell, purgatory and heaven?

Does one automatically have faith by intellectually affirming propositions about these matters? Some would answer "yes" without hesitation. Not only do they consider these propositions to be the contents of faith, but, also, they would go so far as to take certain Aristotelian-Thomistic expressions of these propositions, and even the rather simple question and answer format of the Baltimore Catechism

that was passed from generation to generation, to be the ageless and exclusive expression of "the faith." Thus the preaching is essentially a matter of explaining and defending these truths from age to age and from place to place.

There is a sense in which this is partially true. Clearly the elaboration and beliefs about these ancient Christian concerns are closely related to faith and Christian preaching. Through them faith is expressed, specified and even embodied. However, the example and teaching of Christ, the evidence of Scripture and tradition, the witness of holy women and holy men, and the best of Catholic spirituality and theology strongly attest to the fact that faith, in its fundamental form, is a far more dynamic, existential and personal reality than is conveyed by a somewhat static, propositional and theoretical listing of theological ideas, religious images, Church doctrines or Catholic beliefs.

The fundamental reality of faith is the radical personal and communal response to the unconditional gift of love that the Creator has for each of us. It is this essential movement of Divine life in us that is mediated by the words and symbols of faith, but this spiritual reality is prior to and deeper than our religious words and symbols. Thus "the faith" can never be adequately thematized or verbalized in public discourse. This is why the Church has not only creeds, doctrines and, hopefully, moving sermons but also stained glass windows, deeply moving ceremonies, a rich musical heritage, the rhapsodic expressions of mystics, and a radical social commitment. Thus faith is a response of the whole person — mind and heart. Faith is the ongoing and lifelong response to the call to conversion that is now whispered and now shouted in the depths of a person's very being, and in the unraveling history of a family, a community, a nation and the whole Church.

Faith is a response to the call to conversion, and good preaching nourishes conversion. Conversion is one of those words that has an odd sound in Catholic circles. We usually do not use the word when speaking about ourselves. We use it when we speak of coming forward for Christ at a Billy Graham rally. Conversion is what happens to Christians of

other traditions when they become Catholics! But I am using conversion in a sense that applies to us as much as anyone else.

Conversion is the transformation of the way we experience ourselves, others, the world and the universe. In Frederick Nietzsche's phrase, conversion is the "transvaluation of values." The person who undergoes conversion shall never be the same again. They are turned inside out and upside down by God's Holy Spirit. They are Abram —asked to sacrifice his only son Isaac — become Abraham; Moses before the bush that burns but is not consumed; Saul — knocked from the horse — become Paul; a young Jewish peasant girl become Mary, the mother of Jesus because of her startled "fiat" to the angel's call. They are Simon — prancing in the waves of a stormy sea — become Peter; and perhaps even Jesus of Nazareth triumphing over desert temptations — as the Father's Christ.

In every human person the reality of conversion is a complex of on-going, overlapping elements. The dynamics of the spiritual pilgrimage of faith may be viewed as several different, but related, forms of conversion. Conversion may be religious, Christian, ecclesial, moral or intellectual. You will better understand what I am saying about faith, and what I will say about preaching, if I briefly describe each of these forms of conversion.

III. Religious Conversion

Religious conversion comes about as one becomes aware of what Karl Rahner aptly terms "holy mystery." It is the palpable realization of the religious dimension at the ground of all human experience and activity. Religious conversion is a deeply imbedded sense of the holy or the sacred. It is a tacit awareness of the absolute meaning, purpose and graciousness of one's own life and the entire universe. A potentially mature Christian may be under the sway of this religious conversion even when he or she is questioning or doubting particular teachings or practices of

the Catholic Church. It is possible to be religious in this primal sense and be indifferent to or even in opposition to aspects of institutional religion. Just as it is possible to be an active and seemingly faithful member of institutional religion and be devoid of this primal religious awareness. Institutional and ideological loyalty do not automatically constitute religious conversion. Nor do they automatically constitute faith. Such loyalty, devoid of spiritual vitality is but the simulation of faith.

As we grow in this fundamental awareness, we gradually grasp that the source of our experience of "holy mystery" is not some impersonal energy or blind force but an intelligent, loving, even personal reality. Thus we can speak of God. Through the power of this divine spark at the center of our being, we grasp that life is not so much sound and fury signifying nothing, not a tale told by an idiot.

In spite of the inscrutable paradoxes and seeming tragedies in personal, communal and world history, conversion to God yields the affirmation of the complete intelligibility hidden in the riddle of life. Within this hope-filled horizon prayer enters our lives, and we make our own way with John of the Cross in the Ascent to Mt. Carmel, with St. Theresa of Avila through the rooms of the Interior Castle and with Thomas Merton up the Seven Storey Mountain.

IV. Christian Conversion

To religious conversion must be added Christian conversion. Christian conversion consists mainly in our ongoing response to the question Jesus put to Simon and the disciples. "Who are people saying that the Son of Man is?" In Christian conversion we recognize in the life, ministry, teaching, death and resurrection of Jesus — the presence of the Father's Christ — and thus in Christ we have what Edward Schillebeeckx has appropriately called the sacrament of the encounter with God, Emmanuel, God with us. Christian conversion is not automatic. It is not accomplished instantly by infant baptism or attending church every

Sunday. Christian conversion is not, in the main, a matter of theological theories about humanity and divinity in Jesus or metaphysical constructs about the Trinity.

A person may come to Christ without knowing anything about the great Christological speculations as Nicea and Chalcedon. Christian conversion is a personal appropriation of the paschal mystery. Jesus becomes not a stained glass window figure, not a holy card image, not an emasculated statue on a pedestal, not a coherent doctrine, but a living, pulsating, challenging brother and Lord who walks with you and talks with you and tells you that he loves you. Christian conversion is, as St. Paul says, "to put on Christ". It is to answer Jesus' question ("Who are people saying that the Son of Man is?") with your whole being, "You are Christ, the Messiah, the Son of the Blessed One." Obviously, for the Christian, Christian conversion has a normative place and is not simply an option in the sequence.

V. Ecclesial Conversion

To religious and Christian conversion must be added ecclesial conversion.

Ecclesial conversion is the turn to community. When we are really converted to the Church we realize that religion is not just a matter of "Jesus and me." Under the influence of ecclesial conversion we embrace a living tradition, a community and world family. Ecclesial conversion is not so much having faith in the Church as it is the response to the empowering Spirit's call to *be* the Church, to assemble as the "ecclesia", the people of God. What we believe in is the Creator Father revealed in the Redeemer Son by the power of the Spirit. If Christ is the sacrament of the encounter with God, then the Church is the sacrament of the encounter with Christ, and every Christian is called to be sacrament of the encounter with the Church.

In our day ecclesial conversion must have a special sensitivity to the ecclesial nature of other Christian traditions and our growing movement toward unity. There should be

no more talk among thinking Catholics about "non-Catholics." There should be no more preaching about "non-Catholics." When were we last called a "non-Orthodox"? a "non-Anglican"? a "non-Lutheran" or a "non-Baptist"?

Avery Dulles in *Models of the Church* and a *A Church to Believe In* reminds us that there are many ways of looking at the mystery of the Church. Besides various positive images of the Church as herald, sacrament, servant, mystical communion, and community of disciples, it is possible for a Christian to have an incorrect or at least inadequate model of the Church. Some may conceive of the Church according to a military metaphor with strict rank and control, or as a defensive bastion of a peculiar ideology. Nor ought the Church to be conceived of as an "elevator," a heavenly transport system, that takes us to our "spiritual" destination. We cannot crowd into the Church the way we crowd into an elevator, indifferent to and even suspicious of those around us. If we do, when we get to the top, the Divine Elevator Conductor will declare that "It was the way you treated one another on the trip that counted. So, down you go!" The preacher calls both the individual and the community to ecclesial conversion.

VI. Moral Conversion

To religious, Christian, and ecclesial conversion must be added moral conversion.

Moral conversion is the effort that we must each make to respond to the call of God in conscience. It is the quest for authenticity in every aspect of our lives. Like Socrates, Eliezer, Thomas More, Dorothy Day, Mother Teresa, Dr. Martin Luther King, Jr. and Archbishop Romero, the morally converted person seeks out the good, and does the good simply because it is the good. The morally converted person cares not for appearances, rewards, punishments, advancements or fleeting public opinion. He or she has gone beyond Harvard psychologist Lawrence Kohlberg's five stages of moral development to his sixth stage: the grasp of transcen-

dent values. The morally converted man or woman strives to conform the deeds incarnated in his or her life with the values inscribed in his or her heart. In the effort to achieve moral conversion one struggles with St. Paul, who said to the Romans, "That which I know I should not do, I do, and that which I know I should do, I do not do."

The authentically Christian understanding of moral conversion embraces far more than the sixth and ninth commandments. As important as these matters are, moral conversion is not simply a matter of sexuality, birth control or abortion. Moral conversion encompasses every personal and public area of human thought and conduct where gospel values are at stake. Thus every person of faith must scrutinize his or her attitudes and actions in the areas of war and peace, government, social justice (e.g. racism, sexism), care for the environment, just wages for workers and the horrible prospect of nuclear holocaust from a Christian moral perspective. The Christian does well to be reminded by the authentic preacher that as he or she grows in faith and the moral life, luxurious living quarters, extravagant vactions, an excess of material goods, irresponsible use of alcohol, smoking, indulging one's appetites, overeating, and not exercising and caring for one's health are all instances of moral decline and potential sin. They are not simply minor bad habits to be passed over by rationalizations. The morally converted person should be able to eventually face death saying with Thomas More, "I say none harm, I do none harm, I think none harm. If that be not enough to keep a man alive, then in good faith, I long not to live."

VII. Intellectual Conversion

Finally, intellectual conversion must be added to the others if religion is to be in active dialogue with the modern world.

Intellectual conversion is the slow and painful process through which the thinking person experiences the libera-

tion of intellect and integration of mind. By means of intellectual conversion a person comes to terms with the complexity of the world and the eros of the mind to know everything about everything. It is the realization that things may not be the way they appear. This podium appears solid, but in fact it is a mass of moving particles. Knowing is more than seeing and touching. It appears that the sun rises and sets. But it does not. The earth turns on its axis and moves in an elliptical circle around the sun.

When we open ourselves to intellectual conversion we recognize that there is no one exclusive path to truth: poetry, proverbs, music, art and common sense can all direct one to the true. The findings of serious studies in history, psychology, anthropology, philosophy, science and theology are not necessarily in conflict. By a certain intellectual agility we can appreciate their complementarity. Usually where conflict arises, e.g., so-called Creationist versus Evolution conflict, it is because of the inexact use of language, the presence of bias, misinformation, or issues which simply are not mature.

The seemingly irreconcilable conflicts between Galileo and the Church in a past age are easily reconciled today because a higher viewpoint makes it possible to see that positions that seemed in conflict were actually the result of the confusion of scientific and theological categories. Sometimes it is a matter of just plain error as Pope John Paul II seems to have acknowledged in the case of Galileo and the Spanish Inquisition. Intellectual conversion integrates all forms of human knowing and understanding in a dynamic synthesis. When we eagerly seek God's truth wherever it may be found, we need not be startled when biblical scholars tell us that the infancy narratives are a special literary form. They are not literal accounts of the birth of the Messiah.

There may have been no shooting stars, singing angels, or exotic Magi. But the fundamental theology of the uniqueness of Christ conveyed by the story is, and remains, ever true. The same may be true of the Creation Story in the Book of Genesis. The account of the seven days of creation may convey timeless religious truths through a literary

form, but the literary form may convey implausible cosmology. The general direction of Charles Darwin's theories of natural selection and the origin of the species may be better science than Genesis. After all, Genesis is not a science book. But responsible science does not undermine the religious vision of the Creation Story any more than responsible theology undermines the legitimate advances of science. Without intellectual conversion, many people cannot live with a dialectical view of reality. The capable preacher will be sensitive to his congregation and know when and how to change them in this delicate area of an informed Christian faith.

Intellectual conversion reaches its zenith when we recognize our own intellectual limitations in the face of the absolute mystery of God who dwells in unapproachable light. Due to the limits of language, the historicity of the human race and the permanence of mystery, intellectual conversion must fight arrogance and gnosticism and yield to the light of the Holy Spirit if we are to experience the paradoxical enlightenment that the anonymous medieval mystic termed as the entry into "the Cloud of Unknowing."

Thus the ongoing conversion that feeds the life of faith is religious — the turn to the holy; Christian — the turn to Jesus as the Christ; ecclesial — the turn to community; moral —the turn to values; and intellectual — the turn to a wholistic understanding of truth and human wisdom. Obviously, conversion is not a predictable mechanical sequence. One does not necessarily move smoothly from religious conversion to intellectual conversion. They overlap and compenetrate. Thus, in a particular Christian or Christian community there may exist a very strong loyalty to the Church — a manifestation of ecclesial conversion, but there may be little or no religious sense, or there may be a highly devotional commitment to Jesus as the Sacred Heart — but so exclusive and privatized as to all but exclude the community (marked by indifference to questions of social justice), hence a lack of ecclesial conversion. Again, one may have a highly refined sensitivity to fundamental moral values — authentic moral conversion — but due to certain

radically negative experiences and intellectual questions, a person may think of himself as agnostic, or, even atheistic; that is, little or no religious conversion. This whole process is very different from person to person.

As Harvard's Wilfred Cantwell Smith has said: My faith is different from my brother's. This is a fact. The faith of one of my neighbor's is different from that of another. One can hardly but recognize that Tertullian's faith was different from Abelard's, Constantine's different from Zwingli's, St. Teresa's different from John Knox's, Harnack's different from William Jennings Bryan's. The faith of a Roman martyr was different from that of a hanger-on of the Crusades, and both of these differ from the faith of a modern Bible-belt farmer or Catholic Charismatic. Though faith perdures in the Church, it is in a sense born anew in the hearts and minds of believing men and women each day.

Certainly the faith of these different individuals was nourished by very different forms of preaching.

VIII. Preaching and Faith

In the Catholic tradition the usual preacher is a deacon, a priest or a bishop. And the usual context for preaching is the Eucharist, pre-eminently the Sunday Mass. Many complex elements interplay in the Mass that all have an impact upon the faith development of individuals and the local eucharistic community. Non-verbal and verbal symbols are compounded. The language of poetry, religion, theory, common sense, doctrine and avowal all coalesce without differentiation. They interact with the intersubjective states of individuals and communities in their particular histories and cultures according to their levels of sophistication.

The prevailing ecclesiology and sacramental theology in the Catholic Church prior to the great Council of John XXIII and Paul VI, was so dominated by somewhat static categories and a near mechanistic interpretation of *ex opere operato* that faith would not have been usually addressed in the dynamic and developmental context that I have been

discussing. But certainly the sacraments, particularly Communion and Confession with their promise of an "increase of grace," were considered far more important as sources of spiritual nourishment than preaching. This attitude was manifest in the unecumenical suspicion that often greeted Protestant emphasis upon the importance of the liturgy of the Word (Scripture) and the "sacramental" nature of preaching. Thus generations of Catholics could speak of the "principal parts of the Mass" as Offertory, Consecration and Communion. Therefore if you came late for Mass and "only" missed the sermon you still were not obliged to "hear a second Mass," to use the language of the day.

Happily those days and those attitudes are, for the most part, behind us. All over the country those called to preach are laboring to find creative ways to strengthen their skills as proclaimers of the Word, and more and more Catholic people consider the quality and the depth of Sunday preaching as a key factor in determining their parish affiliation. It is as if there has been a gradual realization that just as the faithful stand before the altar praying that bread will breathe and wine will bleed, that is that bread and wine will give life; so too they stand before the pulpit hoping that the loaf of the Scripture will be broken open by the inspired and living word of the preacher.

Anyone who has delivered or listened to a sermon that truly moved a congregation or to one that simply fell flat knows that there is no set formula or technique for successful and effective preaching. So much depends upon the protein chemistry between the preacher, the congregation, the Scriptures and how these relate to the larger liturgical context and events in the larger community.

But whether you are preaching to a small group of more traditional Catholics at the early morning Mass or to an overflow cathedral at the Christmas Mass of midnight there are certain realities that must be borne in mind. Indeed they must become second nature if the preacher's words are to bear fruit.

IX. Remote Preparation

The preacher who seeks to nourish the faith life of his community must develop the ability to see the "homiletic dimension" of life. That is he must do more than page through 'homily hints' an hour before his sermon is to be delivered. There must be adequate remote and proximate preparation. Remote preparation means more than prayerfully reading the Scriptures and commentaries several days in advance. Remote preparation includes attentive listening to the constructive criticism that the people offer of earlier homilies and actively seeking their suggestions for improving future efforts. It means developing a sensitivity to events in the world, the Church and the local community so as to recognize what might be termed "preachable moments." The Old Testament prophets had the uncanny ability to recognize the tension between their religious tradition and the political and social developments around them. Their prophetic utterances were not so much predictions of the future as they were a two-edged sword: sermons that galvanized the community and confronted them with challenges of practical justice.

The remote preparation of prayer and personal spirituality through which the preacher seeks ever to be open to conversion is essential if the preacher's words are to speak the hard and challenging truth of the gospel. Without this foundation, the preacher can easily become a prisoner of the time and place, preaching values of the culture or the congregation. If the preacher is not spiritually free for the Word to come through him, it will be very easy for him to use beautiful words, weave gossamer images, tell amusing anecdotes and make interesting commentaries without really touching people's souls with the disquieting implications of the Christ-event. When he opens his mouth, the preacher must speak from a great silence.

X. Content, Form and Delivery

To the remote preparation must be added the proximate preparation — that addresses content, form and delivery. Proximate preparation for preaching requires exacting attention to three inner related but distinct elements of a sermon if it is to contribute to the growth of ecclesial identity. These elements are content, form and delivery. In the light of the Scripture, the season of the liturgical year, ongoing events in the community, and the preacher's overall vision of ecclesial life, the preacher must decide precisely what he wants to say and what he wants to happen. While surprise may be very good for the congregation, the preacher should ordinarily not be startled by his own words. Often in a good homily the preacher really only wants to make one, two, or, at the most, three points. The preacher must want to instruct, explain, or clarify; praise, support, or thank; challenge, confront, or convince; console, comfort or commiserate; move, enthrall or inspire. Unless a preacher has a basic idea or intuition of what he wants to happen to himself and his congregation during the homily, he will find it very difficult to determine and control the basic content.

This will be equally true of the form. An essentially didactic homily is cast in a completely different form from an essentially inspirational one. One might have a straight forward and logical development, while the other might be in story format, full of image, affect and deliberate ambiguity. But in either case there can be no wasted elements in the form. Thus while anecdotes, stories, and examples can much enhance a homily, they are useless if they are gratuitous. They cannot be used simply to overcome personal nervousness or to "loosen up the congregation." They must be selected because they in some way illuminate the preacher's message and suggest a practical agenda for the growth of the congregation. The preacher must ever study the rich multi-leveled image in the parables of Jesus which always drive the hearer to deeper and deeper insight. Yet no one ever exhausts their full meaning.

A good indication to me that I have not used examples well is when members of the congregation remember the example but completely miss the point.

Because of the way most of us listen and limit our attention span, the opening and closing lines or paragraphs of an effective sermon are crucial. A well thought out beginning that immediately demands attention and in some way signals all that is to follow and a clear, crisp, confident to powerful ending that brings the point home to each listener makes all the difference. Like the opening and closing notes of the Beethoven 5th Symphony, the start and finish of a homily must be just right. There is nothing more painful for a congregation than sitting through a preacher trapped in the finale of a homily that he cannot simply conclude!

Just as a symphony does not really exist until it is played and heard, so too the content and form of a sermon, no matter how good they appear on paper, only come to life in the delivery. The very same text can be a masterpiece in the hands of a communicator, and a miserable failure in the hands of a mumbler. I should hasten to note that while content and form are always important in preaching, a good homily need not be written down at all. The preacher with a good mind and a good memory and personal discipline need have only the beginning, middle and end outlined in his thoughts to deliver an inviting homily.

Many Catholic preachers seem unaware of a fact that is obvious to most of their Protestant counterparts. Namely, that the human voice is like a musical instrument, and it can be played for many different effects. Rather than using the voice by means of a whisper or a shout, speeding up or down, a pause, a half sentence, to a Joyce-like string of seemingly unrelated words and images to evoke feelings of sorrow and joy, fear and hope, we have tended to simply talk about such feelings. As a result our people might be moved to *think about* certain emotions and Christian realities, but they were not moved to *feel* them. Thus if we wish to end a homily with a ten second line from a poem we should not spend two minutes explaining and even apologizing.

Instead we should simply build up to a climax and declare "God gave Noah the Rainbow sign. No more warnings, the fire next time."

Because of the constraints of western European notions of propriety and restraint the Catholic preacher is usually not allowed to be moved or shaken by the word he announces. He must always be cool, calm, collected and completely in control. As a result his hearers are not likely to be moved or shaken either. They are likely to be asleep. This is probably why we are embarrassed by the black Baptist preacher mopping his brow and shouting "Amen." He does not seem to be in control. Though in fact he is. No matter what our individual style of preaching may be, it is ever true that the pulpit is not the same as a classroom podium. They are different forms of communication. In the podium class it is perfectly acceptable to begin an address with, "Today, let us examine different theories of ecclesiology." Whereas in the pulpit it would be far better to begin, "What is the shape of the Church to come?"

XI. The Competition: Modern Communication

The preacher who wishes to move, inspire and feed the religious life of his people has to realize that he is working against great obstacles. For most people the Sunday sermon is a foreign and anachronistic form of communication in our age of mass media and technology. Most people have no other communication experience remotely like the hour they spend in Church on Sunday.

More and more studies indicate that large numbers of Americans are not serious readers. Unfortunately, the average American is more likely to look at the pictures and captions of *People* magazine rather than read the cover story of *Time*. The forms of communication that are the most powerful are short, clear and uncomplicated: TV commercials, billboards, newspaper headlines, political cartoons, lyrics of popular songs and the plots of soap operas. These forms of communication often have a far greater

impact upon the values of young people, for example, than family, school or church.

Of course, for so many young people, the most dominant form of communication is the motion picture. They spend Saturday night captivated by "Star Wars," "Superman," "E.T.," and "Gandhi" in 70 mm Dolby stereo. Then on Sunday morning they come (or more likely are brought) to church where they are told that the fundamental meaning of existence is being celebrated. The preacher is going to announce "good news" of staggering significance. But what they may actually hear is a droll paraphrase of the *Celebration* homily outline or an appeal for generosity in the Christmas collection.

Obviously the TV evangelists have recognized the audience potential of modern mass communication. While we are rightly uncomfortable with the crass commercialism and pious simplicities of some television preachers, we all certainly must realize that we shall have to find a way of entering into this electronic communication if we are to reach the millions of people who never set foot in a Church. It is not enough to recall those halcyon days when Bishop Fulton Sheen was a household word.

XII. A Personal Synthesis

Preaching that generates life and vision must be born of a personal vision. While almost anyone can give an impressive "occasional sermon," preaching of longterm and lasting impact is the result of a real personal synthesis. If the preacher is intellectually and spiritually alive, he will be aware of the tensions between fundamental human experience with all of its ambiguity, popular religious piety, official Church teachings, the investigations of theologians, the insights of social scientists and the arts, and the concrete demands of pastoral practice and the needs of those who suffer for political, economic, ethnic, racial and sexual biases. He will hold these realities in tension and live in many worlds while he develops a personal synthesis without

yielding to stereotypes of "conservative" or "liberal." The preacher who is deeply committed to the transcendent values of the Christian tradition and the insights of the best contemporary culture will not be wedded to an inflexible ideology. Because of the dynamism of his own authentic spiritual pilgrimage he will have a moving viewpoint that will enable him to appreciate where his people are in their journey to God.

With an awareness of the complexity of conversion — religious, Christian, ecclesial, moral and intellectual — the preacher addresses himself in very different content, form and delivery to the many different audiences: the searching collegians who are unsure of their religious commitments, to the defensively devout who are afraid of change, to those who come to Church out of cultural habit but are in fact in need of evangelization, to those who would undo the foundations of Christianity in the name of relevance and to all those in between.

XIII. Conclusion

Alexander Solzhenitsyn challenged the exhausted West a few years ago in his Harvard commencement address in which he declared that the world had come to a major turning point in its history. He declared that we are at a juncture equal in importance to the turn from the Middle Ages to the Renaissance. It will exact from us a spiritual upsurge. We shall have to rise to new heights of vision and new levels of spiritual life.

Where shall this spiritual upsurge come from? From Government? From Education? From Science? From the Arts? Hopefully members of all of these communities will contribute. But should not the Catholic Church as the largest Christian Church in the United States have a special responsibility?

There can be but one answer. Yes. This responsibility is shared by all the baptized who make up the people of God. But those who serve in public worship play an important

role and preachers are pivotal. Thus our preachers cannot play Moses and hide behind their weaknesses and limitations. Every time we enter the pulpit and open our mouths we ought to have something to say. From a long and deep silence spent in prayer and pondering the Scripture, we must speak words that are food for thought and action in the Church.

Jeremiah speaks to every preacher.

The word of the Lord came to me thus:
Before I formed you in the womb I knew you,
before you were born I dedicated you,
a prophet to the nations I appointed you.
"Ah, Lord God!" I said,
"I know not how to speak; I am too young"
But the Lord answered me,
Say not, "I am too young."
To whomever I send you, you shall go;
whatever I command you, you shall speak.
Have no fear before them,
because I am with you to deliver you, says the Lord.
Then the Lord extended his hand and
touched my mouth, saying
"See, I place my words in your mouth."

Response

Fred B. Craddock

This response to the provocative and evocative paper by Reverend Braxton will consist of four parts. First, I will summarize briefly the content of Rev. Braxton's paper, not in order to reduce or simplify but to facilitate immediate response and discussion. So many and so important are the issues raised here that more deserving engagement of the essay will follow upon its publication. Second, I wish to make a series of affirmations in support of several lines of thought pursued by Reverend Braxton. The third section of this response will be in the form of questions, both substantive and practical, raised by the paper. And finally, I will be so bold as to express a number of cautions to those who would take up the task of implementing the preaching described here.

I. Summary of the Paper

Reverend Braxton's paper was generated by three questions: Does preaching nourish the life of faith of the contemporary Christian Church? If so, what is the nature of such preaching? How is this preaching accomplished? In order to answer the first question, the meaning of "faith" as used by the writer had to be made clear. Two definitions are given.

The general definition which serves to inspire and inform all that follows states that faith is that radical personal and communal response to that unconditional gift of love which the Creator has for each of us. The second definition which functions to provide the conceptual structure for the argument is this: faith is the ongoing and lifelong response to the call to conversion. The key word is "conversion," and surprisingly so, not only because it occurs in a paper by a Catholic scholar, but also because it is regarded as central to the whole subject of growth. Conversion and growth have commonly been regarded as separate and very dissimilar paths to God. For Reverend Braxton, conversion refers to a wide range of faith experiences, no one of them normative for everyone, none of them necessarily dramatic or sudden. He discusses five types of conversion experiences which characterize the faith of Christians. These five are: religious, the experience of the sacred or holy; Christian, the recognition of the presence of God in Jesus Christ; ecclesial, the turn toward the community of believers as the context for Christian life; moral, the effort to make one's actions in private and public arenas conform to the call of God in the conscience; and intellectual, the painful process through which the thinking person experiences liberation and integration of the mind.

Given the variety of conversion experiences which characterize the faith of the members of the Christian community, preaching must be varied in content and form. Preaching can, indeed, nourish such faith but it must be preaching which provides a range of experiences of the Gospel and which treats of topics which present themselves for the "preachable moment," the point where Scripture, congregational life, and the life of the world converge. Naturally, no single formula for preaching will suffice, but the ingredients are always the same: preacher, congregation, and Scripture, all mixed in the context of liturgy and the larger community. Also constant in all preaching occasions is the need for thorough preparation, both the general, which goes on all the time, and the specific, as one works on

a particular sermon. Each sermon is marked by concreteness as to what is to be said and done, being delivered with clarity, passion, and in a voice congenial to the content.

Reverend Braxton concludes with a call to find ways to take the sermon into the world of electronic media, an invitation to preachers to find a personal synthesis while living in many worlds and ministering to a plurality of faith experiences, and a challenge to contribute to the spiritual upsurge so essential in our exhausted generation.

II. Affirmations of Support and Agreement

The following statements, needing little if any elaboration, are offered in support and agreement with several major accents of the paper.

Reverend Braxton properly derives his high sense of the role of preaching in the church not from a "wave of current interest" but from Scripture, tradition, and the congregation's needs and expectations.

Even so, by setting the sermon in the total movement of worship, the paper does not place a burden upon preaching that is neither reasonable nor necessary.

The congregation is not the passive recipient of the sermon but contributes, sometimes even aggressively, both to the content and the delivery.

The preacher's own faith and spirituality are vital elements in effective preaching. For the message to be believable, the messenger should be believable.

Freedom, confidence and passion are not consistently present in a preacher apart from the disciplines of thorough preparation.

It is important to understand that preaching not only *says* but *does*, creates an experience as well as conveys a message. In view of this, sermon form and style of delivery are not peripheral considerations.

Preaching that nourishes is aware of the social, political

and economic as well as liturgical contexts of both speaker and listener. Whether this awareness assumes the forms of resistance, or embrace, or discerning, modification is a part of the burden of preaching.

Preaching that nourishes is appropriate to the listeners' capacities to understand, to believe and to act. The varieties of faith experiences in a congregation cannot be allowed to blur that appropriateness.

III. Questions Raised by the Paper

My first question has to do with the use of the word "conversion." After a brief moment of Protestant pleasure derived from Reverend Braxton's elevation of the word to a place of central significance, I realized he had outdone every Protestant I know in the amount of theological and experiential freight placed upon the term. To be sure, I applaud all efforts to retain and infuse with meaning our Christian words. I resent those break-ins in which good words are stolen from the church's vocabulary vaults and vulgarized on the streets, words such as "charisma," "piety" and "conversion." But sometimes reclamation efforts place too much significance, too many meanings on an old word, making its re-entry into church life awkward if not impossible. "Conversion" may function among us here both to focus and to stimulate conversation, but is it the term by which the church can clarify and celebrate all that Reverend Braxton means by "faith"?

My second question has to do with that type of conversion called "Christian," the recognition of God's presence in Jesus Christ. That this was, of the five types listed, the most briefly treated is understandable. After all, one may assume the most familiarity with this category as expressing the nature and content of conversion. The problem lies in the fact that Christian conversion is offered as one among several types of conversion, none of which is treated as being

of greater or lesser value. Is coming to faith in Jesus Christ as God's presence among us, as the revelation of God's unconditional love, a type of conversion alongside moral or intellectual? Granted, Reverend Braxton says these conversions overlap, but does "overlap" express all that faith in Jesus Christ means, not only intrinsically but also in relation to the other conversions? Without being too narrowly Christological, is it not in keeping with Scripture and tradition to affirm that faith in God as revealed in Jesus Christ is an irreplaceable canon for evaluating other religious, moral and intellectual experiences? I hope I have misunderstood Reverend Braxton at this point. (Editor's note: Reverend Braxton subsequently clarified this point in his paper for publication here, cf. p. 90.)

A final question concerns the category, "intellectual conversion." That the attention given this type experience is more than double that of any other of the five attests to the writer's conviction about the importance of and the need for thinking in the church that is open, liberated and integrated. None can quarrel here. The church must speak and act among the intellectual givens of this century, this decade, this year. The paper laments past occasions when fear, unclear language, and misinformation set the church against the sciences, humanities, and critical methods of investigating texts. But all this is not to say enough about the role of the church in its relation to other avenues for pursuing truth. Does not this discussion portray the church as too passive, standing as a consumer outside the doors of science and art, waiting to see what these others have produced for us to think about? Is not the church also a *producer* of subject matter for thought, bringing to every forum its own understandings of the world, human life and community values? Perhaps I exaggerate my point in order to ask whether Reverend Braxton has not, in calling for a church that is a better *listener* to the sciences, neglected to call for a church that is a better *speaker* to all those whose investigations and discoveries, if unquestioned and unaddressed, could lead to an intellectual distortion of life.

IV. Some Words of Caution

In any paper or sermon, the very act of underscoring certain values inevitably leaves other values, though present and stated, suffering from inattention. Some readers or listeners may become so involved in those matters underlined that they assume nothing else of significance was said. It is the obligation of a response such as this to call attention to some very important items presented but not underlined. The following four statements are an effort to do just that, offered in the form of cautions.

Let those who agree with Reverend Braxton that faith is not only doctrines and creeds and propositions be careful lest they conclude faith is not at all doctrines, creeds and propositions. Christian faith has a memory, and that memory is banked in creeds, doctrines and historical recitations. Anyone who cannot remember any farther back than his or her own birth is an orphan, unequipped to handle truth claims except by visceral authentication and prone to embrace a Gospel captured in subjectivity.

Let those who respond to the call for liberated thinking beware lest liberated thinking be interpreted as the easy, uncritical embrace of the conclusions of the sciences and arts. Resistance and questioning do not necessarily mark one as antiquated and out of date; they are also qualities of the slow and painful path to truth. Each person must earn the credentials of "liberal" or "conservative" and the struggle in the search keeps faith athletic and trim. Otherwise, scientists, researchers and scholars preside as the real priests over the church, accountable to no one.

Let those who concur in the judgment that preaching which nourishes is appropriate to the listeners beware lest their preaching be victimized by that judgment. The Word of God *is* appropriate, it fits, it is *meet* and right. The inappropriate word is at best powerless, at worst, damaging. But what is the appropriate word? An unseasoned and prayerless judgment could lead one into allowing the listeners to become the primary source of the sermon. Sawing the

legs off the church furniture so that it fits everyone may not be the appropriate pastoral act. More appropriate might be exposing them often to the size, to the length and depth and breadth and height of the grace of God which comes from beyond all preachers and all listeners.

Let those who would join in the search for ways to enter the world of electronic media beware lest they be seduced by the giddiness of entertainment and commercialism into which some television religionists have fallen. A world of opportunity is out there somewhere, to be sure. But why not more modest steps for the present? For example, video cassettes and closed circuit television hold enormous promise for the education of the churches. By means of video cassettes the very best the church possesses of sermon, lesson and liturgy can be made available to the smallest and most remote church. And if one thinks of more exposure to the general public, I am not sure but what the mantle of Bishop Sheen could effectively be taken up again. The brevity, the crisp clarity, the thematic unity, the significant subject matter, the gentle courage of those broadcasts might be welcomed as relief from the carnival acts and revivals of superstition which assail us now.

What Is Preaching?
One Heuristic Model From Theology
William J. Hill, O.P.

Response
James A. Forbes, Jr.

What Is Preaching?
One Heuristic Model From Theology
William J. Hill, O.P.

What will be attempted here is something quite modest,
namely, the raising of the question, "What is the preacher
doing when he is preaching?" The burden of this paper,
then, will be one of theological exploration, and the resolu-
tion will be no more than the suggesting of one, tentative
and heuristic theory or model as to what may be going on in
the act of preaching. This is to acknowledge explicitly that
several such theories — all of them viable — are available.
One gain in articulating this one is that it might, in a
dialectical tension of ideas, suggest other viable theories.
This is all the more the case if preaching is acknowledged as
more an art than a scientific task (as would appear to be the
case), for there are no hard and fast rules as to how the artist
sets about his creative making.

To cut quickly to the nerve of the question: the preacher
can be viewed as one who mediates a saving encounter of the
believer with the living God. The locus of the encounter is
the Word of God seen as his utterance towards mankind,
constituting his sovereign and saving initiatives towards
men and women. The context is an ecclesial one, for the
Word of God is spoken to the Church — not to people as

individuals but as persons forming the community of believers. Indeed, God's Word, in its meaning and meaningfulness, is constitutive of that community called Church. Thus, the preacher's word is the Word of God in the form of the Word of the contemporary Church. But — more precisely — what is this?

Some greater precision can be gained in describing preaching or proclamation as "kergymatic re-interpretation or re-presentation."[1] The kerygma is here understood as the content of God's Word brought to language, in a normative way (*norma non normata*), in the New Testament as read in the Church.[2] It is expressed foundationally in Jesus' own message "Repent and believe for the Kingdom of God is at hand" (Mk., 1:15), and more proximately in the Church's message that in the life, death, and resurrection of Jesus of Nazareth, God proferred, and continues to proffer today, reconciliation and salvation to mankind. This, then, is the Word of God — the New Testament being not that Word in a self-identical way, but rather the normative literary articulation of it — wherein even as he (God) must remain concealed, due to man's finitude and his sinful condition, he nonetheless unconceals for us his loving intentionalities towards the world.

All of this is perhaps general enough to be beyond serious controversy. It becomes a bit more problematic with the realization that the *kerygma* — in spite of representing God's once and for all activity that will never be surpassed — does not confront us with one monolithic meaning that needs only to be transferred unchanged into the present, as objectively a finished product that needs but to be translated into contemporary idiom, or updated into today's cultural ambiance. The meaning of the *kerygma* is less somethng enshrined in the texts than something that comes to pass within the consciousness of the believer who reads the text

[1]Cf. W.J. Hill, "Preaching the Word: the Theological Background," *Proceedings*: Catholic Theol. Society of America, 1973, pp. 167-180; and "Preaching as a 'Moment' in Theology," *The Homiletic and Pastoral Review*, October, 1976, pp. 10-19.

[2]First Vatican Council, Denziger-Schonmetzer, 3006-3007.

as God's offer and summons to men and women of today. Such understanding does not occur apart from God's grace and so is an understanding indigenous to faith. But the confession that the *kerygma* is true cannot be made exclusively on the claims of others. We cannot in human authenticity confess that Jesus is the Son of God merely on the grounds that the writers of the New Testament make this claim, or that the Church proclaims it. Someplace in our own consciousness there must be experientially grasped truth (which thereby authenticates itself) on the basis of which the apostolic claims gain credibility, and so make humanly possible the interior act of faith. The question that cannot be escaped is that of Jesus to Peter at Caesarea Philippi, "Who do you say that I am?" (Mt., 16:16).

By the same token, the meaning of the Christian "facts" narrated in the New Testament is grasped by us in what is necessarily a process of interpretation. The would-be preacher brings to the text (and unless one starts here, there is no guarantee that the word spoken is indeed God's Word and not the preacher's own) his own preunderstanding which urges on the text questions which are not identical with those entertained by the original author, nor by subsequent generations of interpreters throughout the forging of tradition. Such preunderstanding comes out of a vast matrix of previous experiences with all the images, models, and conceptual structures in which such experiences have been reflectively interpreted, expressed and so retained. Present experience then (by which is meant experience of reality as it is given to us by God in both creation and redemption) enables the text to yield up nuances of meaning not explicitly grasped before.

This must be safeguarded from any fall into subjectivism or historicism, from any indiscriminate conformity to a prevailing worldly spirit — which would in effect replace the Word of God with the word of men. This is avoided by a understanding that all newness of meaning is yielded up by the text itself. Thus, a dialectical process is at work here; we do not simply confront the past with present experience, but at the same time in a critical way, we allow the past to call

into question our present understanding. In Luther's phrase, echoed today by Hans Urs von Balthasar, it is not that we are to interpret the Word of God, but God's Word is to interpret us. But it interprets us as our situation before God differs historically and culturally from that of believers of previous epochs. Two additional safeguards might be mentioned at this point: (i) the experiences in question are not simply psychological and emotive in kind but cognitive and critical; (ii) secondly, we are concerned with experiences that are not private but rather ecclesial in kind and so subject to the judgment of the Church. They are experiences in the power of the Spirit who "breathes where he will."

Another way of saying this is to note that the Word, precisely as the Word *of God*, over-arches all of history and gathers together past, present and future into the simultaneity and so contemporaneity of the eschatological moment. That means that as the preacher turns to the Word in the lingual expression it has achieved in the New Testament, what should take his interest is not linguistic form or even specific content, so much as its character as God's offer and summons to men and women of today to respond in faith to his proffer of salvation. The Scriptures themselves bring this about, less by conveying to us some specific content than by initiating us into dialogue with their own subject matter (to borrow a thought from Hans-Georg Gadamer) which is God in his saving activity. Our disposition in approaching the texts is one of openness to the call of God (future oriented) which cannot be predetermined and which sounds through the received text.

The text is important because at the same time we are dealing with a Word which is spoken to *men*, and which as such must be uttered historically, that is to say from within a given moment of human history, if it is to be humanly intelligible. Thus, salvation for the Christian is focused on the concrete events which constitute the human life and death of Jesus, and on the disciples' experience of his resurrection. These come to us in the narratives of the New Testament which are already the interpretations by the disciples of their own experience of these events. As the New

Testament articulates their experience in its cultural form, so our own understanding is an articulation of our differing experience of these self-same events. An important difference, of course, is that our experience is mediated by theirs. But it is possible to say that our encounter with the living God, mediated by the text in its objectivity, occurs not only within experience but precisely as interpreted experience.

At this point, a caution needs to be expressed. The task of the preacher is here viewed as one of reinterpreting the content of God's Word on the basis of present-day experience. This is legitimate on the understanding that underlying the language of the New Testament are the experiences of the evangelists (including, of course, such writers as Paul) to which they give expression in the religious culture of first century Palestine and the surrounding Hellenic world. This awareness affords us the hermeneutical key for interpreting our own contemporary experiences, in the cultural categories of the modern world, as instances of God's continuing offer to us of salvation. But this means that the experiences wherein we encounter God are in fact experiences of grace, quite as were those of the inspired writers. They are not *merely* human engagements with the world (whether of nature or of mankind) which are then interpreted only rationally, and so are no more than projections of finite humanity. They do occur primarily as human exchanges transpiring on a horizontal level of existence, but they constitute an experience of reality which amounts to a basic form of revelation. God manifests his presence and his summons in and through the structures of the real, both cosmic and cultural-historical. Religious experience is thus not some isolated sphere of experience, but is a depth-dimension to ordinary experience. But, such experiences are manifestive of the divine only insofar as they are interpreted experiences. There are no "raw" experiences that amount to direct discoveries of God apart from an interpretive element. By this is meant neither an interpretation that is subsequent to the experience, superimposed on it from without, nor one that works a priori determining in advance the meaning of the data, but an interpretation intrinsic and

indigenous to the experience, that forms a dimension of the experience itself.

This is the context of revelation, not because of the experien*cing* as such, but because of *what is experienced* in its objectivity over and against all activity of human subjectivity. It is the phenomena themselves, in their own intrinsic meaning and meaningfulness, as resistant to controlling knowledge on our part, that enables them to mediate God and his will to men and women. Still and all, this is revelatory occurrence only insofar as it is interpreted, because interpretation in this sense is really a response in faith to God's unconcealing of himself through the realities of world and history wherein he draws near to us. This is a faith-act and not one of reason alone because it is a response to the experience of grace, of God proffering salvation to men and women today; in Schillebeeckx's phrase (to whom much of the thinking here developed owes its inspiration), it is an awareness that runs through whatever we experience, that God has made the cause of mankind to be his own (i.e. God's) cause.[3] It is the surrender to truth which gives itself through human rationality but lies itself beyond the grasp of purely rational processes. However, interpretation of this sort (ultimately controlled by the interpreted) has its own history preserved and passed on in living tradition. What is at work here, then, is a dialectical process. The confessional historical faith in Jesus of Nazareth on the part of those of us who feel constrained to preach is the enabling factor in our interpretation of present experiences as themselves revelatory. Yet, simultaneously, that interpretative experience enables us to reinterpret the *kerygma* as God's saving activity towards us today — and in so doing to add to the narration which constitutes tradition.

The significance of all this for preaching is that experience readily gives rise to conviction and certitude due to its self-authenticating character. The experiencer spontaneously seeks to give utterance to what he or she has encoun-

---

[3]Edward Schillebeeckx, *Jesus: An Experiment in Christology*, transl. by Hubert Hoskins (New York: Crossroads, 1979), p. 62.

tered in experience as a witness to it. This is to say that the very experience as something human is bound up with language, indeed, becomes itself a speech-event. The experiencer thus becomes a communicator seeking to draw others into the circle of new understanding which constitutes a faith-response to the encounter with God. The experience thus assumes a narrative structure. Preaching is less the explanation of dogmas or doctrines (necessary as the latter are) than the recounting of a narrative, with all the dramatic implications of bringing to the fore what John Baptist Metz calls "dangerous memories,"[4] and the urging upon the listener of a decision either for or against Jesus as the Christ of God. Putting this into a larger context, the preacher incorporates the articulation of his own new experiences of God's grace into the ongoing narrative that already constitutes living tradition, thereby creatively augmenting that tradition.

This narrative would appear to have two foci, or to unfold in a dipolar way. On one hand is the Christological focus, for the narrative is the recounting of God's rescue of us in the story of Jesus' human life. On the other hand is the Pneumatological, for all genuine proclamation is done in the power of the Spirit. By this is meant the Holy Spirit (*Pneuma Hagios*) who is the Spirit of Jesus crucified and raised, yet at the same time is very God dwelling within us as our spirit, when as in St. Paul's phrase he "lays fast hold upon us." It is the Spirit who inaugurates our experiences of grace, enabling us to believe, not only in summoning us to belief but also in answering that summons within us. The Spirit, however, is characterized by a certain anonymity; He has no doctrine of his own, but "will remind you of all I have said to you" (Jn., 14:26). He conceals himself (as it were) behind the Word who is personally God's self-expression, and has become visible to us in our own flesh. The initial disposition, then, of the would-be preacher is one of surrender to the Spirit who must "not be quenched" (I Thess.,

---

[4]J.B. Metz, *Faith in History and Society*, transl. by David Smith (New York: Crossroads, 1980), p. 200 f.

5:19). It is, in short, conversion, in the sense of that about-face which the New Testament calls *metanoia.*

This reception of the Spirit is at once gift and task. It is God's unexacted grace, but a the same time it is a summons of those in whom it occurs to the mission of witnessing in word and deed to the saving act of God. Thus, the appearances of the risen Christ in the New Testament — which however they are explained, occur in the power of the Spirit — are never without this calling of the disciples to a ministry of the Word. The ever-new meanings of God's Word, then, to which the Spirit grants entree, are, by a dynamic of their own, communicable to others and constitutive of community on the part of those who hear, and in hearing, believe.

This role of the Holy Spirit in forming the community of belief through the Word brings to center stage the work of those who proclaim that Word. What preaching seeks to achieve is: not an institutional or ecclesiastical restructuring (necessary as the need for reform may be there), not Biblical fundamentalism (which fails to take into account the revelatory character of present experiences), not an exclusively charismatic piety (which runs the risk of being merely private, of saying "yes" to Jesus, while remaining resistant to the Church as the community of the Spirit), but precisely the ecclesial reality of a Church truly given over to following after Christ, to seeking ever greater conformity to him and the evangelical values lived by him in his human life. Once again, this is something rooted more in praxis than in theory. But for it the Church needs leaders, and it is here that the role of the preacher is defined; it is to this that the consciousness of the preacher lends itself.

From this, it would seem that the primary obligation to preach belongs to those who hold the office in the Church: bishop, priest, deacon, or minister of the Gospel. But Christian proclamation is truncated and impoverished if such ministerial preaching is not complemented by a vital lay preaching movement alongside it. Significant here is a special obligation, not grounded in office at all but entirely charismatic in origin, on the part of those who belong to

religious orders whose work is apostolic and extends in one way or another to proclamation. The character of preaching here assumes a difference at least in mode. All preaching is Christocentric, and all Christologies acknowledge in some sense the primacy of practice over theory. But for those who live according to the vows of the religious life, this primacy takes the form of a radical following after Christ. Such Christians — to take one obvious example — are impelled through a vow of poverty to a solidarity with the poor, and to a life of witnessing against the tyranny of possessions and the self-assertiveness that motivates it. Here, a concrete way of following after Christ (to the extent that it is genuine) nuances the preaching that it nurtures. Simply put, such preaching acquires a prophetic character precisely because of the style of life out of which it proceeds, one that seeks to correspond in visible and symbolic ways with the radical demands of the Gospel. This is less possible for the institutional Church which cannot so easily depart from the standards of the secular sphere. Thus, the various forms of religious life tend to exist on the outer peripheries of the institutional Church, with an unavoidable tension between them and the domesticated Church. By and large, however, this would appear as a healthy tension.

Be that as it may, the present state of preaching seems to be one of crisis, something not at all unusual in times of major transitions. One way of coming to grips with it is to see it as a crisis of credibility, a lack of deep interiorized belief on the part of large segments of the supposedly Christian populace that forms the preacher's audience. Karl Marx urged his disciples to leave religion alone (by which he meant primarily Christianity) on the grounds that it would soon vanish of its own failed momentum as Marxist societies superseded it. Time has proven Marx to have been very much mistaken. Concern for the God of Jesus refuses to go away. This may point to the fact that the crisis of credibility is not really a crisis of faith but one of culture, i.e. one of communicating the Good News in a radically changing cultural context. I suspect that people *want* to believe but

find the form in which the message is preached alien to their own experiences. Thus, the task of preaching becomes one of forging a new language that is appropriate to those experiences in their revelatory power, without neglecting the normative role of Scripture and Tradition. Jean Paul Sartre has come close to the mark, perhaps, with the devastating criticism that Christianity discredits itself because it makes no difference in the quality of life. Historically, Christians have been quite as responsible for unleashing evil upon society as have non-Christians. Part of the difficulty, at any rate, may be that the way in which Christianity is presented, the mode of its proclamation, has rendered it meaningless in its power to confront present problems.

God is not dead, but it is hard to deny that he is absent from contemporary culture. It is possible that we have been looking for God in the wrong places. What the preacher seeks to discover and to convey, though it is something specifically Christian, is to be found *within* the world rather than outside of or above it. Is not this where the Spirit operates in seeking out men and women, that is, in this secular world even in its very secularity — granted that what is sought there is the Transcendent concerning whom clues are discoverable only at a certain depth dimension of such ordinary experience? If so, then effective preaching will not take place under the misguided notion of fostering escape from the world, for it is precisely from within the prevailing human situation that one will listen for the voice of the Spirit. On the preacher's part, this means a certain solidarity with a wounded world that bears the marks of evil and suffering. This view of things is confirmed if we grant, once again, the primacy of experience in the faith-act. Experiences are by definition always contemporary, for they are an awareness of something in its very presentiality to the subject knowing and so responding in love or in the refusal to love. This is faith in a basic sense as trust that truth lies implicit in the phenomena that confront us as reality given by God, especially insofar as such phenomena are not subject to our manipulations. To use a quite apt phrase of

"Gaudium et Spes" from the Second Vatican Council, "God reveals himself by revealing man to himself."[5]

The very emphasizing of this truth, however, prompts a caution on its understanding and application. Much of the preacher's concern is with restoring life to a Church that has over-adapted to the world and its structures. The life in question here is something specifically Christian — the "new creation" won for us by Jesus in his dying and rising, and lived by us in the Spirit. If this life is mediated to us not otherwise than through worldly realities, it cannot be derived nor inferred from human capacities and achievements. It is always life in response to God's unexpected offer of love, which even while mediated through others, always remains grace from the Spirit. This calls for an attitude of critical negativity towards the structures and the spirit of secular existence, avoiding all conformity to the mores of bourgeois society and conventional piety in the forgetfulness that we are a people of unfulfilled promise. There can be no collapse of faith into ideology; no absolutizing of finite structures of whatever sort, including the ecclesiastical. All such retain a provisionary character.

Another way of putting this is to allow that the prophetic character to preaching bespeaks an element of urgency that attends it. Now is the time, the *kairos*, the eschatological moment in which salvation is offered us. We can even say that the preacher functions in imminent expectation of the *Parousia*; there is a sense in which the Second Coming is already at hand, summoning those who hear God's Word to decision here and now. This forestalls giving to the present order of things a power it does not have. We cannot remain captive to the past, granting our historicity, (though it is there in tradition that the preacher finds his own identity and that of the community he addresses), nor so oriented to the future as to empty out the present of all meaning other than that of being a stepping-stone to the future. Just so,

[5]"Gaudium et Spes," no. 41, the Pastoral Constitution on the Church in the Modern World, Second Vatican Council.

Christian preaching remains aware of the transitory character to contemporary existence, and so seeks the transcending and thus perduring dimension of present life. This is to acknowledge that eternal life is not some mode of duration that merely comes subsequent to temporal duration. Rather, it is the full fruition of what is begun in this temporal existence, the consummation of the self-enactment we are even now achieving in earthly existence. Thus, it is the Kingdom of God already inaugurated within our history but unable to reach consummation except beyond the boundaries of history.

One obvious reaction to this way of viewing the preaching act is that it tends to confuse preaching with theology, especially in light of the dominant tendency nowadays to understand theology and its method as basically hermeneutics. Preaching then appears as a sort of short circuited theological act that moves directly from hermeneutics to communications, from Bernard Lonergan's second functional speciality to the eighth and last of them. To this it must be said that preaching cannot be reduced to a truncated theology; it is much more than a popular presentation of theological views and conclusions. The hermeneutics at work in theology is markedly critical in kind, while that entered upon in service of preaching is more existential and experiential. The priority of praxis over theory is more obvious in preaching, as is the avoidance of technical language proper to theology. The Christocentric element, while proper to both endeavors, engages the preacher less as a Christology of *thinking about* Christ than as Christology of *following after* Christ. I would be reluctant to suggest that ongoing conversion is less necessary for the theologian than for one entrusted with preaching. But conversion for the former serves as reflective understanding whereas it is more immediately orientated towards witness on the part of the preacher.

One consequence of this is that in an age wherein theological pluralism is a *fait accompli*, the preacher is not constrained to commit himself or herself to any one theological system. For example, he or she can view the experiences of

grace as fulfillments of an a priori structure to human beingness (as does Karl Rahner), or contrariwise he can choose to view them as "contrast experiences" of suffering and evil which disclose God as opposing all such abuses of the human (as does Edward Schillebeeckx).

Nonetheless, granting that preaching cannot be reduced to theology, it remains true that the tie is, or should be at any rate, very close. Quite simply, theology is necessary for preaching — if not in the preacher himself or herself, (which would be the ideal case) at least in the ecclesial community. At the very least, theology nurtures preaching, and gives to it a critical base it lacks of itself. Heinrich Ott — in a surprising synthesis of Barthian theology and later Heideggerian philosophy — has concluded, against Rudolf Bultmann, that the continuity here is such that dogmatics constitutes the reflective part of preaching. It might not be claiming too much to conceive of preaching as a "moment" with theology, at least a terminal moment.

And so I have come to an end, having done no more than I promised, namely to suggest one tentative but viable response to the question "What is the preacher doing when he preaches?" Much more remains to be said concerning the varied forms of preaching, the ecclesial context in which it ordinarily occurs, the phenomenon of lay preaching (i.e. on the part of non-ordained), the context of worship and especially that of the Eucharist, the difference between preaching as service to the Church and as service to the world, the prospects offered by team ministry of the Word, the role of prayer in the life of the preacher, etc. The nerve of the theory lies in a re-interpretative act, but one grounded in present experiences insofar as, sustained by and undergone in union with the Spirit, such experiences constitute revelation from God. Since it is grounded in experience, my only hope is that it will serve to stimulate other richer responses in the varied experiences of others.

Response
James A. Forbes, Jr.

Professor Edward Schillebeeckx concluded his book *Christ: The Experience Of Jesus As Lord* with this comment:

> "So, as according to the spirituality of the Tanach and the Christian gospel, salvation from God becomes to its inner consummation in praise and Thanksgiving (b^{e}rākā or eucharistia), and in this praise of God grace in fact expressly becomes the experience of grace, I thought it a good thing to end the book with a b^{e}rākā, and to preface that with the basic ideas of these two books about Jesus in the form of a homily." p.840

That Schillebeeckx should end his monumental christological work in thanksgiving and preaching suggests that great theology should stimulate the homiletical impulse.

It is a mark of my appreciation for the richness of Professor Hill's paper that I gladly confess that my strongest response to it was a desire to preach. But his theology of preaching also raised critical questions about the nature of the preaching task. In the light of his analysis, it seemed wise to put the preaching impulse on hold long enough to reconsider what is going on in the preaching event.

A brief definition of preaching drawn from the paper might sound like this:

> Preaching is the kerygmatic re-interpretation or re-presentation of the Word of God in an ecclesial form and context, in which the preacher mediates a saving encounter of the believer with the living God, through the New Testament message of Jesus as proclaimed in the Church. It is grounded in present experience and is empowered by the Holy Spirit. As such preaching is revelation from God.

This condensed definition of preaching as fleshed out in the paper seems to be broad enough to serve as a congenial basis for ecumenical conversation on preaching. In fact, the surprising discovery from my first reading of the paper was the absence of major points of disagreement with its definitions, perspective or emphases. I found myself eager to join Father Hill in promoting his model of Christian proclamation. Hence, my response begins by sharing what I choose to call points of celebrative agreement. Then I shall yield to the preaching impulse by offering "a hint of a homily" suggesting how this paper challenges our preaching. I shall conclude with some points on preaching for ecumenical consideration.

I. Points Of Celebrative Agreement

The following excerpts or paraphrases from the presentation set forth valuable insights about preaching which I believe will contribute to its revitalization. These twelve stones I have taken from Professor Hill's presentation in hope that I will do no disservice to specific meanings or to the shape of his homiletical model.

- Preaching unleashes the power inherent in God's Word — a power identified as the meaning of God's saving intention.

- Experiences of divine encounter are experiences in the power of the Spirit who breathes where he will.
- Present experience enables the text to yield up nuances of meaning not explicitly grasped before. All newness of meaning, however, is yielded up by the text itself.
- God's Word is to interpret us.
- Preaching is faith response to the encounter with God — a speech event drawing others into the circle of new understanding.
- In preaching we are concerned with experiences that are not private but rather ecclesial in kind and so subject to the judgment of the Church.
- Religious experience is thus not some isolated sphere of experience, but is a depth dimension to ordinary experiences. There are no raw experiences that amount to direct discoveries of God apart from an interpretive element. The interpretation is neither prior to nor subsequent to the experience, but is rather intrinsic and indigenous to it.
- All genuine proclamation is done in the power of the Spirit. The Spirit inaugurates our experiences of grace, enabling us to believe. Therefore the preacher will surrender to the Spirit who must not be quenched.
- The appearances of the risen Christ in the New Testament occur in the power of the Spirit and are never without the calling of the disciples to a ministry of the Word.
- Christian proclamation is truncated and impoverished if such ministerial preaching is not complemented by a vital lay preaching movement alongside it. There are also special moments of proclamation not grounded in office at all but entirely charismatic in origin.
- Life style is the basis of the prophetic character of preaching. Solidarity with the wounded world exposes the preacher to broadened area of power in preaching.

- Much of the preacher's concern is with restoring life to a Church that has over-adapted to the world and its structures.

These elements point us in the direction of life transforming preaching. It is in the spirit of the principles enumerated above that I now venture to offer a hint of a homily.

II. A Hint of a Homily on John 13:17

"If you know these things, blessed are you if you do them." This text is commended to us as we consider the theology of preaching because it calls us to recognize that the fulfillment of the promise of blessedness is integrally related to both knowing and doing. It is an appropriate text for this ecumenical conference because the words of Jesus are offered to us out of a eucharistic setting.

Before the seeds of this sermon can grow beyond the status of just a hint of a homily, there is an exegetical responsibility. We can not fulfill our role of re-presenting or re-interpreting what we have not yet heard in the light of its setting and cultural situation. What is the specific meaning of "these things" in the text? Is the reference to Jesus' instructions (a) about the supper, (b) the washing of each other's feet, (c) a genuine understanding of servanthood, (d) broader and more comprehensive issues of discipleship or (e) some neglected dimension of practice in the early Church. And how are we to understand the blessedness or the happiness which is promised to those who know and do? Furthermore, how inclusive is the "you" to whom the words of our text are addressed. What of God's self-disclosure and intended salvific grace can be mediated in the setting we share at this symposium?

The exegesis is yet incomplete and the fresh interpretation is only in process, yet already several questions and some tentative responses are struggling to consciousness in me. The following outline reflects what I'm experiencing in response to the text in this setting.

In Professor Hill's paper we have been richly informed about the nature of the preaching event. Our text comes to us out of the past and we appropriate for it, and trust that it yields, wisdom regarding the path to blessedness: If you know all this about preaching, blessed are you if you do it. Of course, the formula will break down for want of either knowing or doing. As we work our way toward the full development of the homily, I invite ecclesial consideration of four questions and some responses in the light of what we have heard about preaching.

1)   *Why might our preachers not know these things?*

a) Because the biblical story has not always been represented effectively — there is considerable illiteracy.

b) Because the churches are selective in memory.

c) Because we are sometimes deaf to the questions being raised in our times.

d) Because we sometimes resist the Spirit's urging of a broader grasp of the things to be disclosed through God's word.

2)   *Why might we know these things and not do them?*

a) Because we may know theory and be without metanoia.

b) Because "these things" may appear to be threatening to the system or our institutions.

c) Because there were deficiencies during the days of our formation.

d) Because some may lack the will, skill or power to act in accordance to what they know.

3)   *When might we come to know and to do?*

a) When we find our way back to the table together.

b) When we share more freely what has been revealed to us in our separation.

c) When we re-open ourselves to continuing metanoia and anointing of the Spirit.

d) When we open our ears to the cries of the oppressed and open our mouths and our lives as channels of God's liberating Word-Act.

4)   *How might that blessedness be manifested?*

   a) We will fulfill the prayer request of our Lord (that they may be one, John 17:11) and share his joy.

   b) We will overcome the crisis of credibility (John 17:21) so that the world will believe.

   c) We will discern that our salvation is closer than when we first believed.

   d) We will fulfill our ministry in the world in joy, power and love as we anticipate and celebrate eschatological peace.

I have shared this response to Dr. Hill's paper in confidence that it is the bearer of grace to all of us. But before we can prepare and preach this sermon with full integrity we will need to meet each other in sustained and serious conversation. As we bring our best insights for mutual consideration we must offer them to God as well for sanctification and truth balancing.

Some of the "things" I wish to offer for consideration in our ecumenical conversation are insights I've come to affirm in the communities of faith in which I have been nurtured.

III. Let Us Think on These Things in Regards to Preaching

1) Concern for the renewal of preaching cannot concentrate solely on preachers. If preaching is the Word of God in the form of the Word of the Church, all levels of the Church must be nourished and made literate as preparation for the encounter with the living God through the biblical text.

2) The call to love the Lord with all our heart, mind and soul and strength should caution us against the elevation of any genuine aspect of our human response to the neglect of others. It is inappropriate to promote either rationality, activism, personal piety, or communalistic sensitivity, one at the expense of the other. We are

encouraged to give our all. The proper guidance of the Spirit and the God given leadership of the Church should provide safeguards against reductionisms of form or function.

3) A fresh anointing of the Spirit is available to the Church especially as we come to new forms of obedience and open ourselves to new patterns of service. All who are trained for the priesthood or lay preaching ministries should know what it means to affirm that "the Spirit of the Lord is upon me because he has anointed me to preach the gospel to the poor..." In a broader sense, each member of the body of Christ should know the reality of the Spirit as empowerment for witnessing to the Lordship of Christ and the truth of the Word of God.

4) The ways of God in the life of the Church can never be satisfactorily categorized or routinized. Thus sacramental systems and patterns of ministry must be open to charismatic intervention. The humility to mature within and beyond limiting perspectives of past formulations is a mark of the spiritual church. Preaching need not be locked into the narrow confines of what we have known or done in the past. On the other hand, we must be open to the recovery of vibrant forms from the past as we discern their promise for our times.

5) If preaching is to be understood as one of the events in which the saving encounter with God is to occur, it must achieve a place in the life of the Church which promotes expectations. It is not consistent with biblical understanding to allow preaching to appear to be an unimportant or secondary means of grace. In many churches it will be difficult to give preaching its proper place without expending extra time, money and other ecclesiastical supports, thereby signaling a determination to recover the significance of preaching which our Lord led us to expect.

6) Aesthetic sensitivity and artistic creativity are welcomed in various dimensions of the life of the Church as part of our offering of our best to God. Eucharistic events reflect this desire to aspire to excellence from a human point of view as we experience the beauty and mystery of divine presence. While aestheticism is a potential source of distortion of Christian values, there should be no reason why preaching may not at times be graceful and grace-filled, reflecting our highest art and deepest devotion.

7) Celebration is most frequently identified with the eucharist. But celebration and preaching belong together as well. When preaching has become a celebrative event, the community of faith is convened for genuine moments of liberation. Both Word and sacrament are occasions when heightened attentiveness to divine presence touch deeper dimensions of our lives and call forth freeing expressions of gratitude and devotion. If the Holy Spirit hovers over the worshipping community, the vitality and ecstacy of the divine breath need not threaten decency and order.

May God hasten the day when together we may preach like Peter and Paul. In the meantime, let us accept the challenge of Professor Hill's theology of preaching. Let us share our own perspective with each other as we await God's action to move us beyond inspired theory to blessed practice.

Biblical Preaching As Divine Wisdom
Leander E. Keck

Response
Gerard S. Sloyan

Biblical Preaching As Divine Wisdom
Leander E. Keck

The theme on which I am to speak is intriguing because the Apostle Paul spoke not of the wisdom but of the foolishness of preaching. Yet he did so in a passage which turns upside down the ordinary meanings of ordinary words. In the opening chapters of First Corinthians he asserts that God has made the wisdom of the world into foolishness; to the Greeks who seek wisdom Paul preaches foolishness, whose content is the crucified Christ, the wisdom of God; among the mature he imparts a wisdom which is revealed only by the Spirit. If our preaching of divine wisdom is to be guided by what Paul says here, then we must come to terms with the cross as the heart of what is to be preached, and we must understand the claim that God's wisdom is regarded as folly by the experts in wisdom while it is experienced as God's power by those who believe the preaching. My aim, then, is to grasp the inner logic of what Paul wrote to the Corinthians. The extent to which the problems that plagued the Corinthian church are paradigmatic for our own situation is not self-evident, though I suspect that there is more similarity than we would like to admit. Be that as it may, I shall not undertake to establish that congruence. It is the

rationale of what Paul says and its implications for preaching that I want to trace.[1]

One thing should be noted as we begin: it would be a serious mistake if we were to regard Paul's ideas either as pious, devout sentiments with which we can all agree, or as being so determined by the particular problems in Corinth that Paul's ideas no longer concern us really. At the very least, to understand what Paul asserts ought to elicit from us a serious questioning of our own preaching.

I.

In our passage, Paul concentrates preaching on the preaching of the gospel; he shows no interest in preaching as a way of giving sound advice about living a more fulfilling life. It is the gospel that is the center of attention, and he concentrates the gospel on the cross. For Paul, Christ crucified is both the center and the criterion of preaching. Moreover, he reminds his Christian readers that his own preaching to them had avoided a certain way of preaching, one which, had he pursued it, would have "emptied the cross of Christ." He had avoided preaching which relied on *sophia logou* — a difficult phrase which the RSV renders as "eloquent wisdom," the New English Bible gives as "the language of worldly wisdom" and one for which the Jerusalem Bible simply substitutes the word "philosophy" (and then explains in a footnote that this is a certain kind of philosophy). Whatever Paul had in mind, it is clear that he believed that it was possible to preach in such a way that the cross is emptied of its power, and that there is a way of preaching in which the hearer could experience the cross as the power of God. The alternative is rather stark. Paul does

---

[1]The critical literature on these chapters is vast because the hypotheses have been many. An overview of the discussion is found in Vincent P. Branick, "Source and Redaction Analysis of 1 Corinthians 1-3." *Journal of Biblical Literature* 101 (1982) 251-69. Branick sees Paul using his own, previously composed homily on wisdom (1:18-31; 2:6-16; 3:18-23), which he then adapted for the Corinthian situation (in 1:17; 2:1-5; 3:1-4). Evaluating this proposal falls outside the scope of this paper.

not allow for a spectrum, for a scale of one to ten; it is the bold either/or that he presses. Moreover, according to this passage, preaching makes the cross impotent if it does not expose the prevailing wisdom of the world to be foolishness. Rather than surmise what sort of preaching in Corinth made the cross impotent, we will try to discern how this occurs today — namely, by treating the cross as the climax of a hero story. In order to bring this into focus, we will first reflect on the phenomenon of the hero, and then contrast that with Paul's understanding.

A. To begin with, I will speak of the hero in a much more limited sense than does Joseph Campbell in his important book, *The Hero with a Thousand Faces*.[2] Campbell's net is cast so wide that it includes the protagonist in myth, legend, epic, fairy tale, ritual and art. It is the basic pattern in all this material that he seeks, and which he subjects to a psychological interpretation influenced by Freud and Jung. It is a deep mythic structure which he finds attested everywhere, so that he can write that "the standard path of the mythological adventure of the hero is a magnification of the formula represented in the rites of passage: separation — initiation — return. In other words,

> A hero ventures forth from the world of common day into a region of supernatural wonder: fabulous forces are there encountered and a decisive victory is won: the hero comes back from this mysterious adventure with the power to bestow boons on his fellow man.[3]

By relativizing the particularities of each hero story, Campbell is able to write:

> Whether the hero be ridiculous or sublime, Greek or barbarian, gentile or Jew, his journey varies little in

[2]This book has been reissued many times. Copyrighted in 1949 by the Bollingen Foundation, Inc. of New York, it was published as a Meridian Book by the World Publishing Company in Cleveland, beginning in 1956. The citations are taken from the 15th printing in May, 1971.

[3]*The Hero With a Thousand Faces*, p. 30.

essential plan. Popular tales represent the heroic action as physical; the higher religions show the deed to be moral; nevertheless, there will be found astonishingly little variation in the morphology of the adventure, the character roles involved, the victories gained. If one or another of the basic elements of the archetypal pattern is omitted from a given fairy tale, legend, ritual, or myth, it is bound to be somehow or other implied...[4]

Suggestive as this book is, its psychoanalytic bent causes the author to make assertions about material which go beyond evidence. From the angle of our concern, this is especially true of his absorbing the Jesus-story into the schema.[5]

In the context of this presentation, "hero" is used in a more modest, less literary way. It is not primarily the story line of the Gospels that is in view, but the often fragmentary story line that is present, or implied, in the way Jesus is presented in some contemporary preaching. It is more the image of Jesus as a heroic folk figure that is in view. In such preaching, one usually does not find the pattern of separation — initiation — return, though aspects of it may be present.[6] What one finds is less the archetypal narrative

---

[4] *The Hero With a Thousand Faces*, p. 38.

[5] One can scarcely deny, of course, that Jesus has been absorbed into an all-embracing myth. Indeed, what Campbell describes and interprets — a "monomyth" found everywhere — is what certain forms of (slightly) christianized gnosticism (e.g., the Noasseneo) did already in the second century. The history of Christology shows that they were not the only ones. Mr. John Augustine has called my attention to George de forest Lord's, "Folklore and Myth in *Paradise Regain'd*, in *Poetic Traditions of the English Renaissance*, Maynard Mack and George de forest Lord, eds. (New Haven and London: Yale University Press, 1982), pp. 229-49. Lord sees Milton's poem as a "deeply symbolic version of Joseph Campbell's "monomyth" — one which portrays Jesus as "the ultimate hero of myth." The question is not whether the Jesus-story can be told as a hero's myth, but whether such a portrayal is compatible with Pauline Christology.

[6] One can think of sermons based on the beginning of Jesus' public activity. His leaving Nazareth to find John in order to be baptized would represent "separation," his victorious struggle with Satan in the wilderness would be his "initiation," and the commencement of his preaching would express his "return" to provide boons to others.

which embodies the pilgrimage of our own souls, and more the idealized counterpart.[7]

To begin with, there is no hero without a circle of admirers, whether it be a fan club or an amorphous group caught up in "hero worship." Just as there can be no leader without followers, so there can be no hero without admirers. Indeed, to a considerable extent it is the lionizing done by the admirers that creates the hero by investing him with an aura of meaning. This investiture is a response to achievements which are deemed to be significant. There are achievements which in themselves may be remarkable enough to be recorded in the *Guiness Book of Records*, but it is their deemed significance that transfigures the achiever into a hero. The symptom of this deemed significance is the passion to identify with the hero, to be in his presence, to touch him or to acquire something that the hero possessed. A photo of the hero is good to have; better yet is a signed photo, for the signature — especially if it follows a personal greeting which mentions the admirer by name — announces publically that the admiration is acknowledged; the personal greeting manifests a bond between the admirer and the admired, and suggests that the admirer has access to the hero's mana, of which the out-sized achievements are a sign. In other words, those achievers become heroes whose deeds invite admirers to identify with the doer in order to gain some benefit.[8]

What the admirers expect to gain depends, of course, on the particular hero — whether he is a quarterback with an unerring arm, a popular musician like Elvis Presley, a politician with access to power, or a humanitarian without concern for power, like Mother Teresa. The role of eros and

---

[7]Instructive is the collection of studies of idealized heroes in post-biblical Judaism. *Ideal Figures in Ancient Judaism*, G.W.E. Nickelsburg and J.J. Collins, eds. SBL Septuagint and Cognate Studies 12. (Chico, CA: Scholars Press, 1980).

[8]It should be noted that Campbell's hero, upon returning from his adventures, wants to share benefits. The movement is from hero to beneficiaries. In what has been sketched above, the movement is from beneficiary to the hero, who may not be motivated to be a benefactor at all.

sexual fantasies we can also note without exploring. What concerns us is discerning the unstated, yet powerful, transaction between the hero and his community.

Diverse as these transactions can be, it will suffice to note only two: identification and imitation, both of which involve legitimation. First, *identification*. The admirer identifies with the hero in order to compensate for weakness. Weakness looks for power, ugliness for beauty, ineptness for competence with which to identify. By identifying with the hero who excels precisely where we are painfully deficient, we appropriate the strength, the mana, of the hero in such a way that we live our lives through him. The hero's deeds live my life vicariously, because his excellence compensates for my limitations. This kind of identification is really a matter of sentiment, of romantic fantasy which changes nothing but may well serve as a substitute for change. In *imitation*, on the other hand, hero worship does lead to change because the hero becomes the model, the norm for one's own striving. The admired qualities of the hero become obligatory goals for one's own efforts. Either way, whether by identification or by imitation, the transaction between the admired and the admirer is a form of *legitimation*. The hero validates our wants and values precisely because he achieves excellence which we esteem. He is what we wish we were or strive to be, otherwise he would not be a hero at all. Heroes legitimate because they embody the idealized self. This is why there is a reciprocally reinforcing relationship between heroes and their communities of admirers. By definition, the hero cannot challenge the fundamental values of his clientele; accordingly because heroes legitimate, conflicting, radically disparate, heroes are symptoms of social conflict.

With these terse observations in mind, we ask how one might preach the cross if one's preaching were based on a hero Christology. Right off, one would make rather prominent a certain kind of narrative — one which lionizes Jesus' virtues and emphasizes the miraculous.[9] The narrative por-

---

[9]Such a portrayal of Jesus could be regarded as an aretalogy. A few years ago, New Testament students pursued rather intently, and with strong dissent, the

trait would be of heroic proportions. It would present him as mastering every difficulty and achieving the improbable. The Jesus story would be the account of an achiever, a winner, with whom one would want to identify. In the next place, the heroic Jesus would compensate for the ambiguity and ordinariness of our lives. If we are not well-positioned to take on the establishment, he would do so for us, and we would draw satisfaction from being identified with this fearless prophet. If the ordinariness of our lives and the routine of simple things done among the unimportant people in the world make our own lives appear like minor parts in an obscure play with a short run, then identifying with Jesus puts us at center stage of a major hit. Or, in the third place, one can preach Jesus in such a way as to portray him as the paragon of the self we would like to be. Critic of traditionalism, friend of sinners, articulate spokesman for the will of God, mocker of Roman power, associate of rebels and radicals, lover of children, self-taught poet and teller of tales — he is all of these so naturally that by being more like him in any one of these features we would be better. Either way, Jesus the hero would confirm the values we cherish, for he would embody them.

B. What sort of criticisms would Paul bring to bear on such preaching which treats Jesus and his cross as a hero story? We will note briefly four aspects of a Pauline critique: the anthropological, the christological, the soteriological, and the theological.

First, every mode of preaching Christ has built into it a certain understanding of the human condition, an anthropology, a view of the human condition for which the preached Christ provides a healing alternative. However varied be the forms of Jesus our hero, they have in common

question of the aretalogical character of the Gospels and/or their sources (written or oral). The debate generated considerable literature, intertwined as it was with a Christology which regarded Jesus as a "divine man" (*theios anēr*) — itself a problematic category. The introductory chapter of Eugene V. Gallagher's dissertation reviews the discussion. *Divine Man or Magician? Celsus and Origen on Jesus*, SBL Dissertation Series 64 (Chico, CA: Scholars Press, 1982). Eminently worth reading is Morton Smith's "Prolegomena to a Discussion of Aretalogies, Divine Men, the Gospels and Jesus," *Journal of Biblical Literature* 90 (1971) 174-99.

the view that the human dilemma is essentially one of weakness which can be overcome either by identifying with compensating power or by trying harder to reach a higher standard. Neither is totally devoid of truth, to be sure. Undertaking the discipline of imitating a noble hero does improve one's life, at least in some respects. But from Paul's angle, an improved person is not yet a redeemed self. In other words, from Paul's perspective, preaching Christ as hero settles too quickly for an inadequate view of the human condition as needing mostly more power, a superficial anthropology which assumes that we will become what God intended us to be if we identify with Jesus the hero.

Second, preaching the heroic Jesus in order to elicit identification with the hero would, from Paul's point of view, be seriously deficient precisely where it promises to be adequate, namely in Christology. Paul would say that whoever identifies with Jesus has got it precisely backwards, because the whole point of the Jesus-event is that in it God identified with us.[10] What constitutes the redemptive event is not our establishing solidarity with Christ but is rather Christ's movement into solidarity with us. "Life will be better if you get with Jesus" is one thing, quite another is Paul's word, "He made him sin who knew no sin so that in him we might become the righteousness of God" (2 Cor. 5:21). In the same way, it is one thing for me to live my life through the life of my hero; it is quite another to say that Christ lives his life through mine (see Gal. 2:20).

Third, from the standpoint of soteriology, a hero Christology jeopardizes the cross as the means of redemption —so much so, that it makes a meaning of the cross virtually empty. Serious charges, these. Can they be sustained?[11]

---

[10]In Rom. 8:3 Paul writes of God as "sending his own Son in the likeness of sinful flesh and for sin . . ." Those who, like myself, regard Phil. 2:6-11 as celebrating the incarnation/exaltation and not the attitude of the historical Jesus as an anti-Adam see the same pattern of identification with sinful humanity in this passage.

[11]It must not be overlooked that Paul's emphasis on the cross, if gauged by the evidence of a concordance, is distributed unevenly in the seven undisputed Letters. In Romans, for example, the word "cross" never occurs; only in Galatians 3 does the means by which Jesus was executed play a key role in the argument, and only in

A hero Christology can scarcely avoid seeing Jesus' death as a martyrdom — a consenting death of a good man for a good cause. The deathscene itself can, but need not, be portrayed in heroic terms which emphasize the endurance of agony, the psychological pain of being abandoned by followers, the magnanimity of Jesus toward the penitent thief or the executioners themselves. With or without such features, the death of a hero remains at the level of an example which can inspire imitation. To preach Jesus' death in these terms is to exhort the hearers to be as willing to die for a noble cause as was Jesus. One can appeal to Jesus' own words about taking up one's cross to follow him, and thereby construe the Gospel text to be an invitation to imitate the hero. In this way, "the power of the cross" becomes its capacity to elicit resolute imitation, but that is not what Paul means by the phrase. If the example of the cross becomes mandatory, moreover, then the cross is preached as an obligatory attitude, a requisite readiness to die if necessary. Such preaching of the cross, instead of being the word of God's gracious deed on our behalf, becomes the word of what we must be prepared to do in order to prove that we are serious about our commitments. Thus the word of the hero's cross confirms our assumption that our relation to God will be in good order if we succeed in being like our hero.

From Paul's angle, in such preaching the cross loses its capacity to redeem the hearer from the deeper level of the human condition — bondage, because the hero's cross can be an illustration but not a revelation. At this point it is necessary to make some distinctions, namely between illustration and catalyst, and between catalyst and revelation.

1 Corinthians does Paul emphasize the pivotal importance of the cross in the gospel. Heinz-Wolfgang Kuhn sees three distinct contexts in which Paul speaks of the cross: wisdom, law, and Christian existence. "Jesus als Gekreuzigter in der frühchristlichen Verkündigung bis zur Mitte des 2. Jahrhunderts," *Zeitschrift für Theologie und Kirche* 72 (1925) 1-46 (for Paul, 27-41). Even if one sees the differentiations in Paul's usage, however, one can speak of "the cross" in Paul's thought as a convenient expression for the soteriological significance of Jesus' death.

Illustration makes vivid and concrete what is already known, but it does not disclose reality in a new way or at a new level. Illustration helps to communicate an insight or an idea to the hearer, and so can make speech effective, but the insight itself does not depend on the illustration, for it can be made independently of the illustration; commonly, one has an idea and then looks for an illustration as part of the strategy of communication. The relation between illustration and idea is extrinsic. On the other hand, a catalytic event provokes an insight, provides a disclosure which at the point of origin is inseparable from the insight. In such cases, the truth of the insight may finally stand on its own, just as understanding the law of floating objects does not require everyone to get into the bathtub as did Archimedes, who discovered it there. In such cases, the instance has a catalytic function in revelation at a particular moment. The relation between event and insight is historical but not essential. It still falls short of revelation in the stricter sense. A revelatory event, however, is one which does more than trigger an insight; it becomes part of the insight permanently because it becomes the prism through which alone the insight can be seen. A revelatory event is one to which one returns again and again because it has the capacity not only to repeat the original disclosure but to keep on unfolding its meaning into one situation after another. In this case, the relation between event and revelation is intrinsic and permanent.

When we apply these distinctions, needing refinement and nuancing at every point, to the preaching of the cross, we can see some fairly clear patterns. When the cross is preached as an illustration, it becomes an effective concretion of a principle, such as that good men are often impaled by the system; or, saintly persons are often betrayed by followers whose zeal outruns their understanding; or, resolute undermining of the sanctions of society will get you killed. All of these are true, and we know that they are true apart from Jesus and his cross. Indeed, one can usually think of a series of cases which illustrate the same point, so that Jesus takes his place along side others. It is not illegitimate to appeal to the cross of Christ as an illustration of

something, of course, but one should not confuse illustration with revelation. Likewise, one can grant that at a given moment, the cross of Jesus was the catalytic event which disclosed reality for a particular group in Palestine, long ago. The insight to which it led — the deathlessness of sacrificial love, for instance — can stand on its own. Ever since Immanuel Kant, there have been those who advocate this understanding of Jesus as a whole and not simply for the cross; that is, they contend that the relation between Jesus and Christianity is historical and not intrinsic, that for quite understandable reasons Christianity emerged in connection with Jesus but now that this religion has established itself, it is no longer dependent on Jesus — indeed some have not hesitated to say that it would not really matter if it should turn out that there had never been a Jesus. Even if few would go so far as this, the point is valid — that one should distinguish a revelatory catalyst from a revelatory event which is a permanent fundament, one whose meaning unfolds again and again, so that the result of revelation remains bonded to the revelatory event itself. It is the latter, and the latter only, that Paul has in view in our passage. For Paul, the gospel does not merely have its origin in the event which the cross epitomizes but has its permanent criterion and center in the cross, so that the word of the cross is the means by which that event reaches hearers as a revelation which redeems.

This brings us to the fourth critique which Paul would make of the hero's cross, and this has to do with the relation between the cross and God. In the hero story, God can be very important for the hero, but can never *be* the hero without becoming a demi-god instead of remaining God. That is to say, the hero can be inspired by love of God to endure death, can gladly die rather than compromise loyalty to God, can undergo martyrdom in order to be united with God; in such patterns of understanding, God remains an important reference point for the hero. In all such cases, God is extraneous to the plot. For Paul, however, the story of Jesus' cross is essentially the story in which God is the real actor. The heart of Paul's Christology is formulated in the

remarkable statement that "God shows his love for us in that while we were still sinners Christ died for us" (Rom. 5:8). Paul's gospel, in other words, declares that Jesus' cross is the work of God on our behalf. So astounding is this that the world's wisdom declares it to be foolishness, while those who know themselves redeemed by believing it experience it as the power of God and the wisdom of God.

Insofar as Paul's letters are a clue to his preaching, it is clear that the Apostle has no interest in the cross as the death of a hero, for that would shift the attention away from God's act to the heroism of Jesus, and so would reveal nothing about God which was not known before. We do not know, and cannot know, what Paul knew about the crucifixion. My own surmise, however, is that he would be much more comfortable with the passion story in Mark than he would be with the story in Luke, for it is Luke who comes closest to presenting it as the heroic story of a martyr. In any case, for Paul the salvific significance of the cross does not depend on the preacher's ability to portray Jesus' dying in heroic terms but on what that death discloses about God in light of the resurrection. For Paul, God does not arrive on the scene as the resuscitator of the dead Jesus; rather, in light of the transformation and vindication of Jesus in the resurrection, Paul sees God to have been the hidden actor throughout the event, so that the action of God and the action of Jesus coincide. It is because the story of Jesus and his cross is simultaneously the story of God's love that Paul can conclude that whoever believes this story is rightly related to the truth about God, and so redeemed from trusting a misconstrued God. It was the cross-cum-resurrection that exposed the profound gulf between the truth of God and the prevailing construal of God. Because cross/resurrection as God's act could not be integrated into what passed for knowledge of God, Paul came to see that one was forced to choose between the wisdom of the world and the foolishness of the gospel, and that if the gospel was right, the world's wisdom has been unmasked as folly in the guise of wisdom. Whenever the Jesus story and its cross is portrayed as an

heroic tale of a martyr, the word of the cross is emptied of its power to unmask, and thereby to save humanity from its cherished illusions.

II

Our passage in 1 Corinthians puts also a second item on our agenda, namely, the need to discern why God's wisdom in the word of the cross is deemed to be foolishness by those who need to hear it as good news. According to the Apostle, "the world did not know God through wisdom" (1 Cor. 1:21) — though it is precisely wisdom that the Greeks are pursuing. How is it that wisdom and the quest for wisdom do not lead to knowledge of God, so that when the revelation of God arrives in the word of the cross it is judged to be foolishness? Clearly Paul is not speaking merely of the finitude of wisdom, of its innate limitations — as in the case of a telescope not powerful enough to locate a distant galaxy. What Paul has in view is rather a distortion so profound that wisdom is judged to be folly, while folly is deemed to be wisdom.

Paul does not explain his understanding to the Corinthians, but some time later he did elaborate the point when he wrote to the Romans (Rom. 1:18-32). He writes that because humanity did not honor God as God or give thanks to God, its thinking became confused; as a result, "their senseless minds were darkened." Consequently, he goes on, "claiming to be wise they became fools" and "exchanged the truth about God for a lie" and so they became confused morally as well. Being morally confused, they could no longer gain clarity about God. Illusions about morality reinforce illusions about God, and illusions about God produce illusions about our life together. This is why Paul can write that people use wickedness to suppress the truth. Paul saw what Marx and Freud explained — that who we are and who we think we are shapes how we think of God and determines what we count on from God. This is what

the religious protests of the oppressed have been telling us too — that they see themselves as the victims of our theology, that we will change when our understanding of God changes, for the understanding of ourselves and the understanding of God are correlates.

This is the heart of the matter, so we must linger to reflect more upon it. It is one thing to say, and rightly, that humanity is created in the image of God; the other side of the coin must be seen as well, namely, that humanity images God in its own mirror. This is a far more serious matter than the so-called anthropomorphism by which we image God as a person and speak of God's arms and eyes; it is more serious than anthropopathism by which we speak of God's emotions like joy or anger; it is even more serious than the consequences of picturing God as an old man who is Chairman of the Board or of imaging God as the cosmic Mother. What is at stake is nothing less than what we count on from that mystery we call God, who is the ground of our being and value.

To regard God as the ground of being and value is to discern that, whether one uses the syllable "God" or not, what we regard as the ultimate grounding of what we hold to be true and worth living by, what we regard as the final arbiter of our lives, that to which in the last analysis we know ourselves accountable, is our God. To see it this way is to recognize the possibility that we might base ourselves on something other than God while believing it to be God, or that we live by a gross distortion of God which we take to be the truth of God. To see things this way is to recognize that what the word "God" refers to is not a celestial being about which religious people have some notions as well as convictions, and for whom we must provide a place in our scheme of things in order to avoid embarrassment; rather, "God" refers to the ultimately unavoidable "whence" from which being and value are derived. It is also to recognize that every life and every society implies its "God" because we become like what we trust. This, in part, is what Tillich's dictum formulates: religion is the substance of culture, culture is the form of religion. To put it differently, the much discussed

secularization of the West has not succeeded in obliterating the fact that at bottom what we take to be true and good are matters of religious perceptions, for they are grounded in the Ungroundable which one must simply acknowledge as self-posited.

We may next focus these rather formal and abstract observations and say that God is the ultimate sanction for our notion of justice; that is, God is the final warrant for patterns and systems of distributive justice on which societies are based and which they maintain. At this juncture in our reflections, it does not matter that systems of distributive justice vary, that what one society regards as true equity may differ markedly from what another society regards as fair and just. The point is that what we call "God" is the sanctioner and sustainer of the systems of justice. This is true not only for established systems and for conservative theologies. All reform movements, as well as revolutionary ones, also appeal to this order of things by the very fact that the goal of reform or revolution is aligning human justice. To perceive any system as unjust is to acknowledge that there is a known standard or norm from which the deviance is so great as to be intolerable, just as whoever speaks of illness implies health. Unless one is prepared to follow Epicurus in regarding the gods as indifferent, or to regard the divine as capricious and utterly amoral, one assumes that God is the guardian and guarantor of distributive justice, even if we disagree deeply over its content. Moreover, to see God as the guarantor of distributive justice is to trust that equitable retribution will be the last word even if it is not the present word (unless, of course, God is not able to make good on what is expected — which is to say, unless God is untrustworthy). This is why suffering, be it economic, physiological, or psychological, or a combination thereof, is finally a moral question. This is also why it is common to assume that the moral law is finally consonant with natural law, for both are grounded in the Creator who is the guarantor of appropriate consequences.

We are now at the threshold of another step in our reflections. To speak of God as the ground and guarantor of

appropriate consequences, whether in the domain of the interpersonal or with regard to what is done to the physical world, is to make way for inferring God from results, for inferring the response of God and the character of God, from certain evidence which one regards as the effect of God the cause, be it final or immediate. From Israel's victories one inferred the triumph of God's righteousness; from Israel's defeat one inferred the same thing because the defeat was God's just, punitive response to injustice and idolatry. In other words, if God is the reality that guarantees that there are appropriate consequences for our deeds, then one will also reverse the argument; then one will regard experience as the just consequence of prior action. The biblical experts in this mode of reasoning are Job's friends, who kept insisting that his plight *must* be just recompense. Had they been Christians, they would have appealed to the "unforgiveable sin," whatever that is, because the consequences must have an appropriate cause. When the Book of Daniel was written, the persecution of the faithful called into question the equitable correlation between result and cause, the theology of appropriate consequences; consequently, the first radical theology, apocalyptic, contended that if the saints cannot expect justice in this age, they can count on it in the Age to Come. In other words, the inferability of God survived, because it is near the heart of religion, for it is the correlate of seeing God as the ground of appropriate consequences.

There are at least two problems with inferring God. The one has to do with God, the other with the one who does the inferring. Because they are two sides of the same coin, they must be discussed together. The problem with inferring God is that it compromises the being of God as the Other because it subtly constricts the freedom of God. An inferred God has been deprived of the capacity to stand over against the world, and can no longer say, "My ways are not your ways," for the ways of the inferred God are the ways of the inferrer. God can be or do only what the inferring allows, namely effecting distributive justice which allocates to each exactly what is deserved. The problem does not lie in the inferring

process as such, as if we were forbidden to reason about God; nor does it lie in the notion of distributive justice in itself. What makes the inferred God problematic is the fact that the inferrer has a vested interest which is distorted. In Paul's words, humanity, having gone astray morally, exchanged the truth of God for a lie. We are not to think that Paul was so stupid as to think that anyone deliberately traded the truth for a lie; rather, the exchange was made for the sake of gaining truth which in fact proved to be false. The point is: because the inferred God warrants the self and its values, a self modified by distorted or sinful structures will infer God in such a way as to protect and justify the self in its distortion, or, if the self is burdened by a sense of guilt (rightly perceived or distorted), it will infer that God is the enemy. This is the self to whom the gospel comes as the word of the cross.

Given the distorted construal of God in the name of God, Paul sees that the word which calls into question the inferred God will appear to be folly, not wisdom; he sees that what is truly God's wisdom will be shoved aside as foolishness. He also sees that those who believe this word of the cross know it as both the power of God and the wisdom of God. How will they know this? In a word, they have experienced the rectitude of God as rectification, the holiness of God as sanctification and the power of God as redemption because in believing the word of the cross they know that God made Christ "our wisdom, our righteousness and sanctification and redemption," as 1 Cor. 1:30 puts it. Paul's language is so compressed that we need to reflect a bit more on what is implied here.

In making Christ our wisdom, God made Christ the framework for our understanding of God.[12] In making Christ our righteousness God made him the means of recti-

---

[12]I agree with J.D.G. Dunn, who concludes that the evidence does not support the conclusion that Paul worked with a developed Wisdom (Sophia) Theology —at least not in our passage. Here the divine wisdom "is essentially God's plan to achieve salvation through the crucifixion of Jesus and through the proclamation of the crucified Christ." *Christology in the Making* (Philadelphia: Westminster Press, 1980), p. 178.

fying our relationship to God. Again, what Paul states tersely in 1 Corinthians he explicates in Romans, where the righteousness of God is a major theme. God's righteousness is God's rectitude, God's moral integrity, God's fidelity to the divine character.[13] According to Rom. 3:26, what God accomplished in Christ's death was to manifest God's own rectitude by rectifying those who believe the gospel. That is, God's rectitude comes through effectively not in distributive justice but, as Paul puts it in Romans 4, in rectifying the ungodly. Those who believe the message about Christ's death as God's act find that they are now rightly related to God; they are rectified. Christ and his cross reveal that God's rectitude rectifies. The God whose character is manifested when the word of the cross rectifies the ungodly cannot be inferred from either our well-being or our disasters. The God who rectifies the ungodly can no longer be regarded simply as the guarantor of distributive justice.

In making Christ our sanctification, God made him the basis of that process by which life becomes holy. The holiness of God no longer isolates us from the divine but reaches into our existence in order to make it whole. Just as the right relation to God no longer is the goal of striving but its presupposition, so the hallowing of life is no longer the end product of a rigorous discipline, as at Qumran for example, but the basis of the moral life undertaken in the domain of the Spirit who hallows the everyday by reclaiming it for the Creator. In making Christ our redemption, God's power manifests itself by rescuing us from bondage to the misconstrual of God which is at the heart of sin. Whoever has experienced this by entrusting oneself to God as proclaimed in the gospel knows that the foolishness of God is wiser than human wisdom, and that the cross, which appears to be weakness to the utmost, is indeed stronger than human power because, when grasped as God's deed, it has the capacity to set us right with God.

---

[13]For a fuller discussion of this understanding of "the righteousness of God," see my book, *Paul and His Letters* (Philadelphia: Fortress Press, 1979), chap. 8.

III

It is time to bring our reflections to a head by reflecting on the consequences for preaching. To begin, to preach the cross as the wisdom of God which exposes the world's wisdom to be folly is not to be confused with preaching denunciations of the culture as "so much foolishness." Nor is it to be confused with displaying as normative the preacher's own alienation from one's culture — a temptation which appears to be especially powerful just now. Far too much preaching today claims to be prophetic when it is merely hostile. Nor is the foolishness of the gospel to be confused with the folly of the preacher; so too one must bear in mind that having one's preaching judged to be nonsense does not yet confirm it to be the wisdom of God. All such inferences replace the pathos and note of tragedy in Paul with the self-serving rationalization of the preacher who thrives on rejection and alienation, and whose offensive self-righteousness obscures the offense of the gospel.

In the second place, the preaching of the cross to which Paul has alerted us is at bottom an act of witness to the freedom of God which the preacher has experienced. The surprising freedom of God to rectify our relation to the ground of being and value instead of simply giving us our due is the baseline on which all preaching shaped by Paul will be constructed. Those who know themselves liberated from the illusory construals of God will bear witness to the grace of God in their own lives. They will neither congratulate themselves when things go well, nor torment themselves when they must suffer because the starting-point for their inference about God will be the experienced freedom of God to make things right and not simply to be fair.

In the third place, to preach the cross as God's wisdom which exposed the character of the world's wisdom is to engage in a profoundly theological task. To preach theologically is not to be confused with simply commending theological doctrines. It is rather to identify the understanding of God which is built into the values and life-style of the hearer, and to subject it to a searching critique grounded in the

Christ-event epitomized by the cross. Where the wisdom of the cross confronts the wisdom of the culture, fundamental issues are joined which call for sensitive interpretation of both the world in which we live and the gospel we commend. Preaching which occurs at the intersection of the world and the gospel will be an interpretive event, a hermeneutical act which exposes profound choices which the hearer is invited to make, and to make repeatedly. Such preaching goes far deeper into the issues of life than do homilies which merely exhort a course of action — though exhortation is not excluded. What people today yearn for is interpretive theological preaching which sets out the rationale of the gospel in light of the world's ethos, and which sets out the rationale of the world's ethos in light of the gospel. Unless the inherent rationale of the gospel is set forth so that it makes sense, few will avow it for themselves even if they are in church every Sunday.

Finally, if we take our cue from Paul, who admittedly is not the whole New Testament, we will discover that the gap between theology and ethics begins to close. This is because the response which his gospel elicits claims both the mind and the will, for to entrust oneself to the God who acts in the cross is to engage in a profoundly moral act.

Response

Gerard S. Sloyan

Dean Keck's remarks have been of real help to all of us, both for the central matter he urges us to and the cautions he offers along the way. Our wisdom as preachers is God's wisdom — the cross — or it is folly. The world's wisdom —that very folly — is, at its deepest core, a misperception of God and the divine deed of love. If we press upon our hearers any God but the true God, any Christ but the Christ of God's reconciling act, we are deceivers and leaders astray. There are immense problems in avoiding the pitfall, but it is essential to begin by identifying a false image of God or Christ or the Spirit as the major snare.

A homily's chief purpose is to invite to conversion or recommitment — other ways of saying "accept the divine gift proffered" — hence by definition a homily exhorts. The paradox is, the more hortatory preaching is in spirit or wording, the less likely it is to achieve its intended purpose. Direct invitation to think or act, whether in the old way or in a new way, is easily resisted. We may impress by our earnestness but there are no surprises in store. Preachers, like dancing bears, are expected to perform their familiar routines. This is the worldly wisdom of preachers and dancing bears, which no one need take too seriously. "Good homily, Father." "Fine sermon, Jeannine." Meaning, in the spirit of Gilbert and Sullivan, "And you are wise and I am wise and

we are wise and all the world is wise." A more normal response to the folly of the cross is: "Did she really mean what I thought I heard her say in there?" "What kind of priest have they sent us? He's got the world upside down." If that is the response, it is surely the gospel.

Dean Keck proposes a profoundly theological approach to preaching. He has to be right in that. If the word spoken is no *theologia,* a *logôs toû theoû,* then nothing has been said. The theological is not at odds with the simple, the direct. It is not opposed to the topical, the humorous. The theological is serious, profoundly serious. If, in the pulpit it is leaden-footed, heavy, it probably is not good theology.

I have no problems to report with the splendid suggestions just made in our hearing: to preach in such a way as not to render the cross impotent; to protect the freedom of God and not make God the guarantor of appropriate consequences; to see God not as one who makes all things come around right, if only in the end-time, but as one whose rectitude rectifies. This is a marvelous path mapped out for us preachers. The problem is, how can we ourselves avoid the dangers of invoking an "inferred God" since we are as likely to be modified by distorted or sinful structures as those who worship with us? Dean Keck could be perceived to be inviting us homilists outside the common run of humanity, achieving a transcendent stance that we take to be unflawed both ontically and noetically. I think he is doing nothing of the sort. I think he woud say impatiently, with Paul, "To avoid [such risks] you would have to leave the world" (1 Cor 5:10).

No, he wants us to be very much in the world and fully devoted to denying its wisdom. Anyone who hears us — especially every Sunday — should be moved to do the same. How does one achieve this stance? Is not the church-going believer's chief complaint against the preacher that he — I won't say "she" in this case — is already positioned up there next to God, passing judgments that share in the divine omniscience? If the faithful could quote 1 Cor 4:8 at us they might say: "You are completely satisfied.... You have launched upon your reign with no help from us. Would that

you had really begun to reign, that we might be reigning with you." Any fortification of the clerical tendency to be right with the rectitude of God could push us over the edge. But this is not the invitation we have just heard. It was a simpler matter than that, simplicity itself. We were asked: "Try to get the world straight with Paul." For indeed, like any Christian, "Is it not those inside the community you must judge? God will judge the others" (1 Cor 5:12f.).

The charge just delivered to us is easier said than done, especially to us Catholics who were not nourished on Paul with our mother's milk but came to him — at different stages — later in life. We have to soak ourselves in the thought of this apostle, this great Jew who spent so much time with non-Jewish godfearers, our forebears in faith, in whose unconverted condition we may still be if we have not got his message. That message we just heard: "At the appointed time, while we were still powerless, Christ died for the ungodly. . . . It is precisely in this that God proves his love for us: that while we were still sinners, Christ died for us" (Rom 5:6, 8). That is the marvel that Paul cannot get over. Jew or non-Jew — and that is everyone on the globe —we are the recipients of an undeserved love.

The paradox is that we can be led astray by the very things we most count on as our allies: a knowledge of how God acts in a universe marked by order, a knowledge of how God has acted with the people of the Bible, Israel, a knowledge of the promises made to the covenanted community we know the Church to be. Beware, we just heard it said, of "the misconstrual of God which is at the heart of sin."

I did not hear anything there at odds with the conviction that God is faithful, and will be true to the divine promise. I did not hear a word about a God who because of affectivity is incapable of passing just judgments at the appropriate time. I only heard of a God who went out to us in love, irrespective of merits or race or class or condition, placing one condition only: that we be sinners. Everyone, Jew or gentile, is qualified to be a recipient of that love.

It is not easy to come abreast of the Pauline vision of God. A lifetime of study is not enough. We are not especially

helped by the relative sparsity of occurrence of his seven undisputed letters in the new lectionary. Even the common lectionary under the sponsorship of the Committee on Common Texts — a U.S. and Canadian venture, the results of which we look forward to, will I think disappoint us. The great Pauline affirmations simply are not very often made in a three-year period. There must be ongoing study of the Pauline letters by the preacher, both in privacy and in the company of others. Our conviction of who the God is who has acted on our behalf, and how, must be purified. St. Paul does it incomparably. Help is available from other quarters. Surely Paul was not the only Christian, a title which Nietzsche awarded only to the one who died on the cross. Reading some of the Fathers, some of the mystics, some modern poets helps. We need to cultivate a great idea of God if we are to have a true idea of God. The danger is idolatry: the predictable God, the God who must respond in our fashion, the God of solid inference. If we have not experienced God acting freely on our behalf, we cannot proclaim the wonder. The Christ-event epitomized by the cross must have subjected *our* lifestyle to a searching critique first — it must have interpreted us and our culture to ourselves — or we will have nothing to say.

Just a word about the props and assurances which Dean Keck seemed to rob us of, some of our most cherished homiletic possessions. I mean Jesus our exemplar in suffering; Jesus the archetypal pilgrim through life, to follow whom is true discipleship; Jesus the innocent just one, the Jewish martyr whose death the evil one achieved. But notice what he was at pains to affirm and to deny: to deny that Christian existence is, above all, a matter of doing, to *affirm* that it is chiefly a matter of the prevenient grace and love of God. The first gospel of human striving "makes sense." The second is utter folly. Even our cherished role as cultural nay-sayers was taken from us. When I heard it said, "Far too much preaching today claims to be prophetic when it is merely hostile," that word was directed to me. Our speaker left us all naked, in some measure. That is a good start. Now we can begin.

The Catholic tradition in theology and preaching is large-ly based on the synoptics, I should think, with Johannine themes interspersed not as an independent witness but in the spirit of Tatian in his *Diatessaron* — namely, a misguided complementarity. Our need to come abreast of Pauline riches does not require the repudiation of some very old and solid conventions among us. Matthew, for example, was the prince of the Tridentine lectionary who gobbled up Mark like Pac-Man; Luke, too, in the Q material they have in common; whenever he could, in fact, except for the Lucan parables of mercy, the first two chapters of Lucan prologue, and the programmatic statement of Jesus in the Nazareth synagogue (Lk 4). Much of that imbalance has been recti-fied in the new lectionary, provided we do not let ourselves become Tatian's *redivivi* but share with our hearers the special gift of each evangelist as a witness to the one gospel of Jesus Christ. In their diversity is the church's treasure: the multiplicity which Irenaeus felt he had to justify without, it would appear, appreciating the fruitful tension among the four gospels.

Matthew has a christology of Jesus as the wisdom of God unlike any other New Testament writer. Jesus does not only make an exposition of Torah more dependable than any teacher. He is for Matthew the wisdom of God embodied. I do not think he is precisely the messianic Torah of rabbinic expectation — an instruction which will be easy to abide by in the final days. Jesus Christ in Matthew is the wisdom of God revealed to humans enfleshed in this teacher. I think the title "a new Moses" is wrong. It makes Matthew replace the Lawgiver, which is the last thing he wishes to do with Jesus. Jesus is the guide to perfect fulfilling of the Law. Cleaving to him is living by the very wisdom of God. I think M. Jack Suggs covered well what Matthew was up to in his *Wisdom, Christology and Law in Matthew's Gospel* of a dozen years ago (Cambridge: Harvard University Press, 1970). It is a wonderful help in comprehending the depths of our Catholic Matthean heritage and keeping us from igno-rant anti-Jewishness in our treatment of the antitheses of the Sermon on the mount. I quote Suggs' concluding phrases:

As envoys of Christ, the incarnate Wisdom, the disciples are charged with the responsibility of being good scribes — of "teaching the commandments," of "binding and loosing," of being "salt and light." — This is not to say that... the preaching of the cross stands outside their range of duties as envoys of Christ.... They are Wisdom's [capitalized] "prophets and wise men and scribes" (Matt 23:34).

Suggs then describes the Jesus of Q — the sayings common to Mt and Lk — as wise man and "child of wisdom," a mediator of divine revelation. "The Jesus who meets us in Matthew... is no longer merely a prophet (albeit, the last and greatest) of Sophia. He *is* Wisdom and that means, as well, that he is the embodiment of Torah" (p. 127).

Dean Keck in a footnote agrees with James D. G. Dunn in *Christology in the Making* (1980) that St. Paul did not work with a developed Wisdom (Sophia) Theology — at least in 1 Cor 1-3. Here the divine wisdom "is essentially God's plan to achieve salvation through the crucifixion of Jesus and through the proclamation of the crucified Christ" (p. 178). This claim of Paul's as to what the divine wisdom consists in does not invalidate all other New Testament wisdom christologies. I have referred to those of Matthew, in which Catholic preachers are peculiarly at home, and Q — in which their more educated hearers, on whom the niceties of the Cappadocians culminating in Chalcedon are lost, are likely to be more at home than they.

This does not say that the wisdom christology of the Johannine prologue — continued throughout the fourth gospel without the term *logos*, "word," standing for *hokmah*, the divine wisdom ever at the Father's side which has become flesh in Jesus — is generally unavailable to today's congregations. It is available to them if it is made so: in powerful Christmas morning homilies, where the prologue occurs each year; in every occurrence of a Johannine reading, where Jesus Christ is the wisdom of God come down from above, especially in the dialogues with the Samaritan woman and Nicodemus and the Jerusalem crowds. We are

suffused with the wisdom of God in human flesh in the Johannine readings, with this assurance:

Amen, amen I say to you, whoever accepts the one I send accepts me, and in accepting me accepts the one who sent me.

This is, indeed, the chain of transmission that brings the wisdom of God into human lives.

We could spend the rest of the morning reflecting on the preacher as theologian, as sage, as purveyor of the wisdom of God. I am profoundly grateful to our speaker that we got as far as step one: the beginning of wisdom is not the fear of the LORD our God but fear of faithless misconstrual of God — which is our great enemy as heralds of the gospel.